Southern Literary Studies
Louis D. Rubin, Jr., Editor

Thomas Wolfe Interviewed, 1929–1938

Thomas Wolfe Interviewed 1929–1938

Edited by
Aldo P. Magi and Richard Walser

Louisiana State University Press
Baton Rouge and London

Copyright © 1985 by Louisiana State University Press
All rights reserved
Manufactured in the United States of America
Designer: Joanna Hill
Typeface: Century
Typesetter: G & S Typesetters, Inc.

Grateful appreciation is extended to Paul Gitlin for permission to print excerpts
from an unpublished letter by Thomas Wolfe to Marion L. Starkey (in the
Special Collections of the Mugar Library, Boston University) and to reprint a
passage from Thomas Wolfe's *A Note on Experts: Dexter Vespasian Joyner* (New
York, 1939). Copyright © 1983 by Paul Gitlin, Administrator C.T.A., Estate of
Thomas Wolfe. Reprinted with the Estate's permission.

Library of Congress Cataloging in Publication Data

Main entry under title:

Thomas Wolfe interviewed, 1929–1938.

   (Southern literary studies)
   Includes index.
   1. Wolfe, Thomas, 1900–1938—Interviews.
2. Novelists, American—20th century—Interviews.
3. Fiction—Authorship.   I. Magi, Aldo P.
II. Walser, Richard Gaither, 1908–   .   III. Series.
PS3545.O337Z8633 1985   813'.52   84–25083
ISBN 0-8071-1229-1

10 9 8 7 6 5 4 3 2

Contents

Contents

Illustrations

Preface and Acknowledgments

Thomas Wolfe, more than any other American writer with the possible exception of Walt Whitman, revealed himself in practically everything he wrote. His feelings about his craft, about his family and friends, and about his America are clearly evident throughout his work. The interviews in this collection, all but a few long buried in newspaper files of the 1930s, provide a further view into Wolfe's character.

Apparently, Wolfe usually was eager to meet with reporters and was generous with his time even when such interviews interrupted his writing schedule. One of the most attractive aspects of the interviews is their immediacy. Wolfe's answers to the questions were of necessity given on the spot and therefore were unpolished. He was always polite and, to avoid giving offense, might say one thing at one time and a variation at another time. In Atlanta, for example, he was "anxious to read *Gone with the Wind*"; five days later in Raleigh he told a newspaperman, obviously in joking reference to his own lengthy novels, that he had told the Atlanta folks, "Hell, I haven't got time to read a book that long."

He was capable of capricious, though harmless, untruths. In 1931, he told Marion L. Starkey that when he was compared with Walt Whitman after *Look Homeward, Angel* was published, he sought out the poet, whose works "were largely unfamiliar to me." Five years later in the May Cameron interview, Wolfe affirmed that he had "never read Walt Whitman" until after the publication of his first novel, thus denying that he had studied Whitman in school. It is an insignificant untruth, but an untruth nevertheless. Like many writers of fiction, Wolfe indulged in exaggeration and trivial fabrication if minor deceptions contributed to the making of a good story. The influence of Whitman is very clear in his later writing but not stylistically evident in *Look Homeward, Angel*.

In the interviews as published here, a few significant factual errors that might be mistaken for truth are followed by corrections in brackets. For example, Sanderson Vanderbilt and the *Rocky Mountain News* both reported that *Look Homeward, Angel* was written in 1930. Vanderbilt's erroneous statement that the novel was written in Switzerland came from a hasty and faulty reading of Wolfe's early draft of *The Story of a Novel.*

The interviewers frequently disagreed about minor details. All, however, tended to remark on the color of Wolfe's eyes, the abundance or sparsity of his hair, his impressive figure, and of course his height. (Thomas Wolfe was six and one-half feet tall.) They often reported on his southern drawl, his manner, and his way of speaking.

In the interviews there are, not unexpectedly, many recurring topics. Wolfe's answers to anticipated questions which were repeatedly, and understandably, posed by interviewers often took on a playback sound, as though he were equipped with half-memorized responses to certain expected queries. He was always ready to defend autobiographical fiction, to tell about Scribner's acceptance of *Look Homeward, Angel,* and to report again and again his astonishment at Asheville's reception of the book. He liked to supply information about his youth, his education, his trips abroad, and his life in New York City. He seldom tired of naming his favorite books and authors. He was fond of reciting the number of words he had written, the number removed from his published novels, and the number he was then writing. Because nonacademic readers as well as scholars have a distrust of ellipsis points to indicate omissions, we have retained Wolfe's repetitions.

Nowadays we have become accustomed to lengthy interviews with writers, recorded on tape, transcribed, and usually submitted to the person being interviewed for revision. Such interviews, frequently done by other writers and by scholars familiar with the author's life and work, are in effect demiessays, which can present in depth and with considerable authority the views of the author. The interviews with Thomas Wolfe in this collection are very different. The products of several hours of questioning at most, they were put together from jotted-down notes and from the interviewer's memory of what Wolfe said—sometimes, we suspect, more of the latter than the former. Although the plausibility of the journalists is impressive, readers should keep in mind that Wolfe's comments and observations set in quotation marks must be accepted as the approximate, not necessarily the absolute, words spoken.

These interviews, we feel, are not sacred writ. Though the verbal texts are unaltered, retaining not only Wolfe's repetitions but also routine biographical facts which the reporters thought their readers should be told, typographical slips have been corrected, and to provide consistency, adjustments have been made in punctuation, italicizing, and spelling. We have made these adjustments because we wish the selections to be relatively uniform in presentation.

From 1935 on, Wolfe was interviewed in cities where his fame had preceded him. Whenever the information was available, we have identified the local interviewers. In our headnotes we have endeavored to provide the contexts of the occasions for Wolfe's meetings with the reporters and in our afterwords to follow through on what later transpired.

For their cheerful responses to numerous requests while these interviews were being collected and edited, we are especially indebted to the following: David Herbert Donald, Elizabeth Evans, Leslie Field, Jesse C. Gatlin, Jr., Clayton Hoagland, Richard S. Kennedy, John S. Phillipson, Ann S. Smith, Theodore V. Theobald, the Braden-Hatchett Thomas Wolfe Collection, Reg Degan and Todd Dudley of Memphis University School, and the reporters and publishers who are acknowledged in footnotes to the separate interviews.

Chronology

1900   Born October 3, in Asheville, North Carolina, the youngest of seven living children of William Oliver Wolfe and Julia Westall Wolfe.

1904   Traveled with his mother and sister Mabel and brothers Fred and twins Ben and Grover to St. Louis. Mrs. Wolfe operated a boardinghouse, the North Carolina, for six months during the World's Fair. His brother Grover died of typhoid in St. Louis.

1905   Entered the Orange Street (public) School, Asheville.

1906   Mrs. Wolfe bought the Old Kentucky Home (Dixieland of *Look Homeward, Angel*) in Asheville and began to maintain a boardinghouse.

1912   Enrolled in the North State Fitting School, a private school operated by Mr. and Mrs. J. M. Roberts. Mrs. Roberts sensed young Wolfe's writing talent and encouraged his literary inclinations. In later life, Wolfe called her "the mother of my spirit."

1916   Entered the University of North Carolina at Chapel Hill, where for four years he achieved success as a gifted and well-rounded student, a dramatist, a writer, and editor of the campus newspaper.

1917   Romance with Clara Paul, the Laura James of *Look Homeward, Angel*.

1918   Did civilian war work in Norfolk, Virginia, during the summer. Brother Ben died of influenza at age twenty-six.

1919   Won the Worth Prize in Philosophy for his essay *The Crisis in Industry*, printed as a pamphlet by the University of North Carolina.

1920   Graduated with a B.A. degree from the University of North Carolina. Entered the Graduate School of Arts and

Sciences, Harvard University. Studied playwriting with George Pierce Baker of the 47 Workshop.

1922   Received M.A. degree from Harvard. Father died in Asheville, June 20. Returned to Harvard in the fall to work with Baker for another year.

1924   Began teaching English in the Washington Square College of New York University. In October sailed aboard the *Lancastria* on his first trip to Europe, landing in England.

1925   Visited Paris, traveled in France, Italy, and Switzerland, and returned to England. In August sailed home aboard the *Olympic*, where he met Aline Bernstein. Resumed teaching at New York University in the fall.

1926   In June sailed aboard the *Berengaria* on his second trip to Europe. Traveled with Aline Bernstein in France and England. Settled in London and began work on *Look Homeward, Angel*, then called "The Building of a Wall." Made first visit to Germany in December. Returned home aboard the *Majestic*, arriving in New York December 29.

1927   Continued work on *Look Homeward, Angel* for six months, then in July sailed aboard the *George Washington* on his third trip to Europe. With Aline Bernstein, traveled in France, Germany, Austria, and Czechoslovakia. In September, sailed home aboard the *Belgenland*. Resumed his teaching at New York University.

1928   Completed the manuscript of *Look Homeward, Angel* and engaged Madeleine Boyd to be his agent. In June sailed aboard the *Rotterdam* on his fourth trip to Europe, landing at Boulogne. Traveled in France, Belgium, and Germany. In Vienna received a letter from Maxwell Perkins expressing interest in *Look Homeward, Angel*. Sailed home from Naples in December aboard the *Vulcania*.

1929   Scribner's accepted the novel. Resumed teaching part time while revising the manuscript. "The Angel on the Porch" was published in *Scribner's Magazine* in August. Made a short visit to Asheville in September. Resumed full-time teaching.

Look Homeward, Angel was published October 18. The book caused an uproar in his hometown.

1930   Stopped teaching at New York University. Awarded a Guggenheim Fellowship in March. Sailed aboard the *Volendam* in May on his fifth trip to Europe. Traveled in France, Switzerland, and Germany. Settled in London in October.

1931   Sailed home aboard the *Europa* in February. Rented an apartment in Brooklyn and wrote a variety of material.

1932   Broke off his affair with Aline Bernstein. "A Portrait of Bascom Hawke," published in *Scribner's Magazine* for April, tied for first place in a $5,000 short novel contest.

1933   Finished first draft of *The October Fair.*

1934   Worked with Maxwell Perkins on revision of the novel. Engaged Elizabeth Nowell to be his agent for periodical publication.

1935   Sailed aboard the *Ile de France* March 2 on his sixth trip to Europe. *Of Time and the River* was published March 8. Visited Germany, where he was lionized as the great new American writer. After two weeks in Copenhagen, sailed home aboard the *Bremen*, arriving in New York July 4. Participated in the Writers' Conference at Boulder, Colorado, June 31 to August 7. Toured the West for the first time, returning by way of St. Louis. *From Death to Morning* was published November 14.

1936   *The Story of a Novel* was published April 21. Bernard De Voto's attack "Genius Is Not Enough" appeared in *Saturday Review of Literature* in April. Sailed aboard the *Europa* on his seventh and last trip to Europe and attended the Olympic Games in Berlin. Visited Austria with Thea Voelcker. Sailed home September 17 aboard the *Paris*. Quarreled with Maxwell Perkins. Left New York December 26 for trip to New Orleans. Met William B. Wisdom.

1937   From New Orleans traveled to Atlanta, Raleigh, and Chapel Hill. In March "I Have a Thing to Tell You" was serialized in the *New Republic*. In mid-April left New York for a brief,

first trip to Asheville since the publication of *Look Home-
ward, Angel*, with stopover visits in York Springs, Pennsyl-
vania, to see his father's family, Bristol, Tennessee, and
Burnsville, North Carolina, to visit his Westall relatives.
Arrived in Asheville May 3, where he was treated as a ce-
lebrity. Left Asheville for New York on May 15. Returned to
Asheville July 2 and rented a cabin at nearby Oteen. Left
Asheville in September, spent several days in Roanoke,
Virginia, and returned to New York. Broke with Scribner's
and signed contract with Harper's.

1938   Continued to write feverishly on his new book before handing the unfinished manuscript to his new Harper's editor
Edward Aswell. Left New York for Purdue University to
deliver a lecture on May 19. Began Far West tour with
visits to Chicago, Denver, Portland, and Seattle. In June
made a two-week tour of the national parks with Raymond
Conway and Edward Miller. Became ill in Vancouver. Hospitalized in Seattle during July and August. After two
operations at Johns Hopkins Hospital, died in Baltimore on
September 15. Buried in family plot at Asheville.

Thomas Wolfe Interviewed, 1929–1938

New York University *Daily News*, October 29, 1929

Eleven days after the publication of Look Homeward, Angel, *the New York University* Daily News *at Washington Square College, where Wolfe was then teaching, ran on the first page an interview titled "Thomas Wolfe, W.S.C. English Instructor, Author of Much Acclaimed First Novel." Guy Savino, student assignment editor, who had decided to write the story himself, was led by the long-legged novelist to a Scribner's bookstore on lower Fifth Avenue. From there they went to 27 West Fifteenth Street, where Wolfe's unkempt quarters were often visited by Aline Bernstein, the Broadway stage designer who was Wolfe's benefactress and mistress.*

This first of many Wolfe interviews was reprinted in the Thomas Wolfe Newsletter, *III (Fall, 1979). The ellipsis points are in the original.*

Referring to *Look Homeward, Angel* by Thomas Wolfe, a Washington Square College English instructor, whose book was recently published by Charles Scribner's Sons, Thomas Beer said: "It is the most important contribution to American Letters since Glenway Westcott's *The Grandmothers.*"

"Among the first novels that give me an impression of strength and promise," wrote Harry Hansen in the *World*, "is *Look Homeward, Angel*. There is rich emotion in it, there is understanding in it . . . it becomes a formidable book . . . Mr. Wolfe's commendable strength makes criticism seem captious."

In Sunday's *New York Times* book section, Margaret Wallace wrote: "Here is a novel of the sort one is too seldom privileged to welcome. It is a book of great drive and vigor . . . is as interesting and powerful a book as has ever been made out of the drab circumstances of provincial life."

Preliminary reviews indicate Scribner's have found a worthy successor to Ernest Hemingway's *A Farewell to Arms*. Praise from critics is not necessarily a criterion of success, but all things being equal

it may be New York University has among its instructors the writer
of what may develop into a best seller.

Thomas Wolfe fails of seven feet by inches. He is far taller than the
average person and walks as though he has difficulty in forgetting he
is not walking through doorways. He has long black hair, combed
back in pompadour fashion. His feet and hands are big. In the W.S.C.
English office he more than fills his chair, and the space beneath his
desk falls far short of sufficing for his legs. So he lounges in the chair,
his legs sprawled over the arm rests in comfort. His voice is marked
by a Southern drawl.

"You will have to ask me questions. I've never been interviewed
before," he said in a measure too boyish for his measured tones, for
the immense size of his body. "*Look Homeward, Angel* is my first
book. I want it to go over—big. It only came out recently and I
haven't received many reviews as yet. I hope it is liked. I worked
hard on it. I wrote it in a little sweat shop on Eighth Street. A real
sweat shop it was. I roasted in the summer and I froze in winter.
That was not so bad. I was always afraid I was going to be burnt out.
The flats below me and over me were vacant. On cold nights tramps
came in to stay for the night. I didn't object, but I tried hard to keep
them from smoking. I wrote the entire book in longhand. There are
over 600 pages to it now. That means over 250,000 words. I suppose it
is not short like other modern books. The publishers cut away 200
additional pages when they revised it, which is just as well, I suppose, though every word they sheared away hurt like the dickens.
I was in Vienna when I heard it was going to be published. I rushed
home, of course, and I have lived at Scribner's, almost. They don't
seem to mind. They say some authors don't even bother to read the
reviews of their books. Imagine!"

Seven-foot-minus Thomas Wolfe, flushed of cheeks and bright of
eyes, glowing with anticipation that held both hope and dread, made
the task of imagining an author blasé about his books impossible. He
wrote his gem into large ledgers. The number of them filled a trunk.
He wanted to show them. He didn't live far from the school, he said.

Thomas Wolfe led the way up Fifth Avenue. No mistaking that the
book is his first. It has filled every part of him, and until it is ac-

cepted or rejected by the public, he will be always seeming ready to leave his skin. He began writing the book in England, though he got the idea in New York City. No, not in New York City. It began when he was a student in North Carolina. It grew when he went to Harvard. It grew when he came to New York. He was ready to thrust himself on paper in England. Walking about in the musty fogs, the story grew and grew on him. He wrote part of it, then rushed home. He finished it in the Eighth Street sweat shop.

Threading his way across Fifth Avenue, exclaiming he would never be able to accustom himself to New York traffic, he explained why he came to New York to finish his book.

But first he saw Scribner's window of books. "Look. My book is displayed in that window. It is in the center. There it is, the one with lightning bars all over it. They placed it in a nice spot, didn't they?" His eyes came away from the window unwillingly.

Then he said he had returned to New York because the high speed of life here is a splendid aid to real work. In a big place like this you can lose yourself, he said. You can be as lonely as you like. The best hours for writing for him, he said, were from twelve to five. *Look Homeward, Angel* grew between that period. It took twenty months to complete the work.

His home was off Fifth Avenue. "My housekeeper," he said, "shows up only three times a week. This is one of the days she doesn't." Up the rickety stairs, two flights, then a turn to the right. The home of Thomas Wolfe.

It is a big rambling room. It is a combination bed and dining room. Also it is a parlor and living room. In a corner are shelves massed high with books. He pointed out a trunk of ledgers. They lay in a jumbled heap. A student in one of his classes typewrote the manuscript for him. He typed several hours each night.

The author knows of what he writes. "I was born in the South," he said. "I am just twenty-nine years old. I think I will stay at this age. I was graduated from North Carolina University in 1920. I was editor of the *Tar Heel* while I was there. It is nothing as pretentious as the paper here. Still I had a lot of fun doing the work.

"While I am not exactly a disciple of the modern school, my book is part realism and part fantasy. I have tried to make it real. Some say it is an answer to Sinclair Lewis' *Main Street*. Perhaps it is. I did not write with any such intentions. As I say in the foreword, *Look Homeward, Angel* explains life in a provincial city as I saw it."

Guy Savino pursued a career in journalism, becoming president of Leader Newspapers, publisher of five weeklies in small northern New Jersey communities. Almost half a century after the interview, his recollections of the occasion appeared in all five (for example, the Commercial Leader *of Lyndhurst) on November 16, 1978. He added some details, recalling that when he arrived at the "cubby hole" that served as Wolfe's office, "There I found a man with a proud but different smile on his olive-skinned face, a great shock of black, unruly hair, a celluloid collar and a stringy tie. Wolfe arose. A better description is Wolfe uncoiled. He lifted himself up from his chair and he rose like an elevator, the full six feet six inches of him. . . . 'Thank you for coming,' said Wolfe in a staccato voice. He seemed almost to stutter in his haste to dislodge the words. 'I think it would be better to go to my place.'"*

First, the two of them walked up Fifth Avenue to Scribner's. "Wolfe regarded the window with undisguised joy. 'Isn't it just wonderful!' he bubbled. 'Isn't it all so fine!'" Back downtown, just as they were ascending the steps to Wolfe's "abandoned loft," out of the door came "a plump, round-faced little woman," who "was about to get into a Packard sedan when she saw us. Wolfe introduced us. It was Aline Bernstein. . . . In the loft I was able to see the ledgers in which Wolfe wrote longhand. There were dozens of ledgers scattered on the floor and filling at least one trunk. We talked and Wolfe handed me a shot of whiskey. It was Prohibition. 'Don't tell, don't tell,' cautioned Wolfe with a grin. Wolfe gave me an inscribed copy of Look Homeward, Angel."

Savino reported that sometime later he wrote "so ferociously" and enthusiastically about the novel in the Commercial Leader *that his Catholic pastor became alarmed.*

Asheville *Times*, May 4, 1930

One of Wolfe's favorite passages in literature was the moment in Tolstoy's War and Peace *when young Prince Andrei, after his first battle, observed that praise was heaped upon those who had done nothing and blame upon those who had done everything: "Prince Andrei looked up at the stars and sighed; everything was so different from what he had thought it was going to be."*

Wolfe had a similar experience in which everything was different from what he had expected. More than money, more than nationwide applause, what Wolfe had wanted most from Look Homeward, Angel *was approval and acclaim in his hometown. He had written the book with affection for his family and his people, and he believed his offering would be accepted with admiration and pride. The book was his justification of a life spent among those closely and strongly allied to him.*

But instead of approval and acclaim, Asheville's citizens expressed outrage that a native son had probed into the secrets of the town, had crucified his family by portraying them as grotesque, and had left the townsfolk with not a shred of dignity. No matter that the book received the plaudits of critics in New York and elsewhere. Back home Wolfe was condemned by those whom he had most wished to convince of his worth. Look Homeward, Angel *was published in October, 1929. Six and a half months later, the town still seethed.*

"Wolfe Denied 'Betraying' Asheville—Claims Love for People in 'Look Homeward, Angel'—Intentions to Cast Reflections of Asheville and His Own People Denied; Will Sail Saturday for Europe" was an "exclusive dispatch" by Lee E. Cooper, a reporter, recently of Asheville, who had interviewed Wolfe in New York.

A weary giant of a man, surprised at the success of his first book, and considerably troubled over the critical comments it inspired among his home folks, will sail from New York next Saturday for Europe "to sit on a rock and gaze at the pigs and peasants, the sky and the sea," so that he may rest.

Tom Wolfe cannot rest in New York. He has had but little time he could call his own since *Look Homeward, Angel* was published. Conferences with his publishers about his next book, chats with literary lights and book critics, invitations and letters have kept him on the go for weeks. But after a brief period of relaxation he will finish *October Fair* and perhaps fifteen or twenty other novels in time, he says. Some parts of his next book and much of those which may come later will be based on his experiences in Asheville and western North Carolina. He hopes that the people he knows back there will like his later works better than the first, and come to understand his motives and his attitude. But he doesn't expect to prostitute his writing because some people have heaped calumny and threats upon him or to weaken what has been generally acclaimed as a promising literary debut by describing life "with a coat of molasses."

Physically Tom Wolfe is a worthy product of the great hills which nurtured him. In an ordinary New York apartment he would be smothered; so he has lived one flight up in an old building on West Fifteenth Street, not far from Fifth Avenue, where one great room, half studio, half loft, with a double-height ceiling, has served as his library, bedroom and reception hall. It was even more dishevelled than his heavy crop of dark hair. Books and papers were strewn all over the place, waiting to be packed away. It was with evident pleasure that he greeted one who could talk with him of places and things in the Carolina mountains.

"I am happy and flattered that *The Asheville Times* had the enterprise and thoughtfulness to inquire as to my attitude on the things I have written about," he said. "I want the people back home to understand. I gather from what some of them have said about me since the book was published that they feel I have betrayed them, that I am an outcast and that they do not want me to come back.

"If they think I intended to cast reflections on my old home and my own people they have gone far wrong. I started *Look Homeward, Angel* about three years ago while I was in England and while I was lonely for a sight of my own land. The experiences of my early years welled up within me and cried out for expression. The result was a book which represented my vision of life up to the age of twenty. I intended the town which was its setting to be a typical town and I called it Altamont, a place which some folks later identified as Asheville. I came back to New York and worked on the novel for many months in a dingy loft on Eighth Street. During all that time I don't believe I actually thought of Asheville as such for more than an hour.

"But I had to write of things which were a part of me, out of my own experience, things which I knew. I don't believe that a worthy book can be produced by anyone who attempts merely to reach up into the thin air and pluck from it a story which has no background of life.

"To me the characters in my book were real people, full-blooded, rich and interesting; they were pioneers of the sort which has built this country, and I love them.

"I am proud of my family, and I still consider Asheville my home. New York certainly is not. I like it, but it is a giant of steel and stone far different from the open spaces where a man can plant his feet on caressing earth and breathe. Only recently I took a trip down to Pennsylvania, to the Lancaster farm lands where my father lived and which I recognized from the vivid descriptions he had given me early in my youth. Part of me belongs to that country, and another part is bound up in the hills of North Carolina.

"When I write, I must write honestly. Too many have tried to imitate the gentility of the English, when we in America are different, without the lengthy background which makes their writing fit the setting, and therefore makes it real. We are pioneers, builders, and vigorous ones, too. To write of such with too much gentility is dishonest, unsatisfying. If we are to get anywhere surely we must paint life as it is, full and deep. Not all of it is sugared, sinless. If that were true, perhaps we would be less attractive, less worthy of being written about.

"The people in my novel were real people to me, and I loved them. Perhaps some sanctified ones will hold up their hands in horror and exclaim: 'Poor devil! So that's the kind of a man he is and that's the sort of person he likes!' but I repeat I love that type—the rich, honest, vigorous type.

"Some writers like Sinclair Lewis have missed the meat of the small town, anyway. Although people recognized his characters, his towns were painted as drab and dull. I do not consider them so, I mean the typically American towns. Life is there in all its fullness.

"I have received hundreds of letters, some praising, some filled with advice, some with abuse," he continued, pointing to a large trunk filled with them. "Many were from Asheville. I hope the people there will get to see my point of view and will like my later books better. I am not bitter and I don't want to be considered an exile, for I want very much to go back there some day."

Tom Wolfe was happy to explain just how his first novel got its name. Few who have read the book seem to have understood the significance of the title.

"As has been the case with many books," he said, "the title finally chosen was not the original one. When I submitted the manuscript to Scribner's I had it entitled 'People Lost' to express the theme of the book and the idea that people largely are lonely, seldom get to know each other. The publishers, or rather their sales promotion department, didn't like this, on the ground that it told too much.

"I submitted about a dozen more titles which wouldn't tell too much or would be likely to arouse curiosity as to the content of the novel, as they suggested. One of these was 'Look Homeward, Angel,' taken from Milton's Lycidas, the full line reading 'Look Homeward, Angel, and Melt with Ruth.' The poem, as you doubtless know, is an elegy written in memory of a friend who was drowned. The application was intended to be general or symbolic in meaning, rather than to have a definite implication concerning some character or action in the book.

"Some persons have thought it had direct reference to the angel which stood on the porch of the marble shop in one scene in the novel, but such is not the case. I think it fits in rather nicely with the character of Ben, perhaps the central figure in the book, who always is jumping up to ejaculate 'Listen to this,' or some kindred expression as if he were conversing with some unseen spirit."

Mr. Wolfe's book will be published in England this month. After a few weeks of rest he will resume work on *October Fair* on which he already has done considerable work. The Guggenheim fellowship, amounting to about $2,500, awarded to him on account of his first book, will allow him to spend several months abroad, mostly in England and Germany. The award is a most generous one, with few strings attached, although the winner usually is expected to go abroad. No accounting to the fund is required.

There will be no definite setting for *October Fair*, he explained. Mostly it will be a moving panorama of American life. The action in the first part, to be entitled *The Fast Express*, will be laid in a fast train traveling through Virginia, and in the territory through which the train passes. The title of the book, which brings up a picture of harvest time and its bounty, will have reference to a period in the life of a woman. Some parts of the story will be based on his experiences in North Carolina. Later books will contain even more of those experiences.

Tom Wolfe has a voracious appetite for studying life and literature. At Harvard, while studying playwriting under Prof. Baker, he wrote several plays which were deemed quite promising, at least one of which he hoped would be taken by a New York producer to make the rest easy. But after waiting for several months in Asheville for such a bid, he lost his illusions and came to New York University to teach. Every time he managed to save up a few hundred dollars he hurried away to Europe, sometimes coming back in steerage. He estimates that out of the past seven years he has spent at least three in Europe. But always he gets lonely for the "spaciousness" of America and the larger grapefruit on the street vender's cart.

He has read and taken to heart all the advice and the criticism of those who have written him letters. Some have asked him in effect why he didn't write a story about good people, a clean story about the beauty of things. He answers that life isn't like that at all, that it is neither clean nor dirty, but full, rounded and sweeping, "like a wave breaking over you."

Thus he talked for two hours, sometimes with a rush of words which left him almost breathless, again haltingly, as if groping, abashed at the inadequacy of mere words to convey the depth of his meaning or his enthusiasm for life.

He doesn't agree with those skeptics who always fear that the promise of an author's first work may not reach fruition in later writing. At least he doesn't think it will apply in his case. He says so without appearing boastful, for he believes that he has learned things since he started writing *Look Homeward, Angel* which will help him to do better.

"I am going to write a good book some day," he says.

Then he poured himself another cup of tea, and began to talk again about the people he knew back home. "Grand people," he called them, "and some day I shall go back there. Tell them that for me, will you? Tell them I mean it with all my heart when I say they are the heart of America."

Wolfe was pleased with the interview, but not with an unsigned article in the same issue of the Times: *"Marble Angel Loved by Wolfe's Father in Riverside Cemetery—Statue Made Famous in 'Look Homeward, Angel' Stands Vigil over Grave." Accompanying the article was a photograph of the "angel, chiseled of finest Carrara marble . . . her right hand lifting a wreath to a rustic cross." According to the reporter, the angel had once looked "eastward" from the "shop porch" of stonecutter W. O. Wolfe on Pack Square. Now it "marks the grave of a departed Asheville woman, buried in 1914."*

The news story was, of course, ridiculous. In The Story of a Novel *(New York, 1936), 23–24, Wolfe wrote about a "scene in the book in which a stonecutter is represented as selling to a notorious woman of the town a statue of a marble angel which he has treasured for many years. So far as I know, there was no basis in fact for this story, and yet I was informed by several people later that they not only remembered the inci-*

dent perfectly, but had actually been witnesses to the transaction. Nor was this the end of the story. I heard that one of the newspapers sent a reporter and photographer to the cemetery and a photograph was printed in the paper with a statement to the effect that the angel was the now famous angel which has stood upon the stonecutter's porch for so many years and had given the title to my book. The unfortunate part of this proceeding was that I had never seen or heard of this angel before, and that this angel was, in fact, erected over the grave of a well known Methodist lady who had died a few years before and that her indignant family had immediately written the paper to demand a retraction of its story, saying that their mother had been in no way connected with the infamous book or the infamous angel which had given the infamous book its name."

It was not until 1949 that Wolfe's angel—"poised upon cold phthisic feet, with a smile of soft stone idiocy . . . the carved stipe of lilystalk" in her hand—was discovered in Hendersonville, twenty miles south of Asheville's Riverside Cemetery.

Lee Edward Cooper, graduate of Duke University, was city editor of the Asheville Times *before joining the New York* Times *in 1929 as real estate editor. On May 10, six days after the interview appeared, Wolfe sailed on the* Volendam *for Europe.*

Boston *Evening Transcript*, September 26, 1931

Marion L. Starkey was so impressed upon reading Look Homeward, Angel *that she was determined to meet its author; and since she wrote occasionally for the Boston* Evening Transcript, *she arranged with the newspaper to go to New York to interview Wolfe. Several weeks after the piece appeared, Wolfe wrote to thank Starkey for her "nice letter and the copies of the interview." He would need no more, he said, for a Boston friend had sent "an enormous package by parcel post which must have contained 50 or 100." He praised the interview: "I can't imagine how much patience and work it must have taken to give order and coherence to my torrents of talk. I only wish I could really express myself as clearly and plainly as you made me talk. And if you really wrote each word between hay fever sneezes—then I think some of the rest of us must try to catch the disease." He regretted her inability to get in touch with him on her recent stopover in New York and, with more legibility than was usual for him, gave her his telephone number and Brooklyn address. "Please let me see you next time," he pleaded. "Goodbye for the present and good luck to you all this year. I have been invited to the University of Va. late in Oct. but don't think I can get away. I'm working away as usual and don't like to stop it now. With all good wishes for health and success—Yours Sincerely." (This letter is in the Special Collections at the Mugar Library at Boston University.)*

The article, "Thomas Wolfe from North Carolina—A Young American Writer Who Leaped into Fame with His First Novel," was accompanied by a profile drawing of the novelist.

Two Octobers ago the mountain city of Asheville, North Carolina, awoke in considerable excitement to find herself celebrated in the 600 pages of a gargantuan novel called *Look Homeward, Angel*. A first novel by an unknown, the twenty-nine-year-old Thomas Wolfe, a former Asheville boy, it was no ordinary novel to be skimmed through and forgotten. Critics were to acclaim it, Sinclair Lewis was to find occasion in his Stockholm speech in acceptance of the Nobel Prize to hail its author as one of the most promising writers of America. But what excited Asheville was not that it had produced a possibly great author, but that it had produced a writer who had written in embarrassing detail about Asheville.

He had not, to be sure, called it by name. He had disguised it as "Altamont." But to anyone with the slightest acquaintance with the Carolina highlands, Altamont was vividly and unmistakably Asheville. And it was such a portrait as could not easily be quoted in pamphlets prepared by the Chamber of Commerce to advertise the "land of the sky." Not that it was satire, after the manner of Sinclair Lewis. It was a straightforward, almost naively truthful and complete revelation of the beauty and ugliness of life and humanity as experienced by a boy growing up in the mountain city.

And what most excited the populace was the fact that readers of *Look Homeward, Angel* thought they could recognize literal portraits of various citizens. Indeed, they say that streetcar conductors still point out to strangers where this character or that character lived. Whether that is true or not I do not know, but when I visited the place last June, an official of a bus terminal named to me two or three characters who he assured me were flesh and blood citizens and pointed out the spot in the square where he said the marble angel once looked out from Gant's shop to the Great Smoky Mountains.

All this was very astonishing to the author, who never dreamed that his home town would fairly buy out an edition, and who denies that he painted any such literal portraits of the citizenry as the town maintains.

"I thought that if three or four copies of my novel were sold in Asheville it would be doing well," said Mr. Wolfe. "It never entered my head that people would read it as they did, that they'd take it so literally and get so stirred up over it. But I heard plenty from the town! There were even a few threatening letters, anonymous, of course.

"People persisted in seeing resemblances between characters and real people where none was intended. In writing that novel it was as if I were a sculptor who used the clay from a certain place in order to create a figure. People from that place could correctly say, 'I have seen that clay before,' but they could not truthfully say, 'That figure is familiar to me.' That was the mistake Asheville made. Because it knew the clay so well it insisted it knew the figures also.

"Lately, I understand, the excitement has subsided. People have taken a juster, more rational view of the matter. And Asheville has been having troubles of her own. I don't know which I feel the most keenly—sympathy for the total collapse of its boom projects, or admiration for the splendid courage with which it is facing the closing of its banks and its hard times."

This talk took place in a little library in the office of Charles Scribner's Sons on a sweltering midsummer afternoon. Mr. Wolfe, who has recently returned from his year abroad on a Guggenheim fellowship, is now living in Brooklyn, trying to whip into shape for publication the manuscript of another mammoth novel, *October Fair*. He had been at work on it all the morning, knocking off just in time to come in from Brooklyn to be interviewed.

I had no difficulty in recognizing him when he stepped forth from the elevator on the fifth floor. There couldn't possibly be two of Thomas Wolfe. This writer of Titans of novels is himself a Titan, six feet four in height, a brown-eyed, dark-haired giant. And as he talked in the little library I was to find him a sincere, rather serious young man, inexhaustibly patient with the demands of his inquisitor. His experience, I gathered, is roughly parallel to that of his hero, Eugene Gant. Not that you can take *Look Homeward, Angel* literally as an autobiography. But its author, like his hero, was educated in the University of North Carolina at Chapel Hill, called Pulpit Hill in the novel, and he seems to have shared some of Eugene's wartime experiences at Norfolk, Newport News and Langley Field, Virginia. The novel ends with Eugene's intention of studying for an M.A. degree at Harvard. At this point Mr. Wolfe's own story may properly begin, for he did go to Harvard and remained there three years.

"New England was wonderful to me—is wonderful still. In fact, right now I'm looking for a place on the Maine coast to rest awhile this summer," said he. "I think it is common for Southerners to have a longing, almost a homesick longing, to see New England. If there is any bitterness left as a result of the Civil War, I haven't experienced it.

"For myself, I think it was partly the New England winters that attracted me. Our winters in Asheville are not exactly mild, to be sure; we have snow, but not as New England has it. To me, studying there at Harvard, there was something fabulously beautiful about the snow. There is a feeling in the air before the coming of a snowstorm, almost it is a smell of snow, which affects me powerfully. Then when it comes and footfalls are deadened I feel as if I should be happy if it snowed forever. I feel that I never write as well as I can on a snowy night.

"But of course there were other experiences in those three years around Boston. I was overwhelmed at that time with an insatiable, an almost cruel appetite for literature and life. I couldn't get enough of the one or the other. I wanted to read every volume in the Widener Library, and simultaneously I wanted to be out with people, seeing them, understanding them. It has taken me a long time to adjust my life to the demands of these two almost contradictory desires.

"I studied in Professor Baker's workshop, wrote plays, had no idea then that I wouldn't dedicate the whole of my life to writing plays. All that ambition seems strange and far away now. When I finished his course I had a play which I confidently expected to see produced on Broadway. It concerned a Southern city and contained a sensational scene between a white boy and a colored girl. I think it was called *Welcome to Our City*.

"It was shown to some producers in New York, who were so cordial in their comment that I went home to Asheville in the calm certainty that I would presently be sent for to help in its production in New York. But instead came a kindly rejection, and I went to New York not to produce a play but to find work. I became an instructor of English in New York University.

"Teaching I found hard work. It looks easy, only three or four days a week, a few hours a day, but it is a kind of creative work and demands a concentrated energy. I found that so many hours of teaching exhausted me in very nearly the same manner as so many hours of writing. After three hours of teaching I found writing a real effort. I was also troubled sometimes by the question of what there is in English that can be taught. Certain mechanicals can, of course, but what else I am not sure. I know people who say that in English they are teaching people to think, but I can't understand how that can be. Why, if I knew where such a course could be found, I'd certainly take it myself!

"Teaching literature is another problem. I have been alarmed by the attitude of some of my teacher students whose habit was to assume as dogma that certain poems are fine and others are not. Some would insist that Gray's Elegy is beautiful, not because they had had personal experience of its beauty, but that they had unquestioningly accepted the dogma that this poem is beautiful.

"Discipline and order is of course necessary in education, and yet I sometimes wonder if there isn't too much of it. I remember that when I was in college and found difficulty in mastering a subject of no natural interest to me I was told that this was knowledge that would help me later in life. But experience has taught me that this painfully acquired knowledge leaves me and is useless to me, whereas the knowledge that I have acquired through sheer enthusiasm has remained.

"My years at New York University were happy ones. I found interesting minds among my students and colleagues, and the authorities were kind. Whenever I had money enough I would cut away and go to Europe. When my money was gone I would return and they would take me back. My associations with the university extended over about seven years, though that didn't come to more than about three years of actual teaching. Most of the rest of the time I spent in Europe. I learned this curious thing about myself in those years of wandering, and I think it is true of Americans as a whole. We're a homesick people, homesick for something we haven't here, and homesick still when we seek it abroad.

"Americans are never naturally still. I remember how in childhood I used to see people sitting on the porches in Asheville in their rocking chairs, always rocking back and forth. I think there is some secret significance in the American fondness for rocking chairs, in being able to move about even while they rest. The rocking chair is perhaps a symbol of that restlessness which is in our blood.

"The automobile has been like a more improved variety of rocking chair. It is another symbol of restlessness, of homesickness for we know not what. People get into the car, and drive thirty miles to the next town to get a soda. There is no beauty in that next town, nothing that they haven't at home, but just going there satisfies a craving.

"Abroad I found Americans wandering as restlessly. A few claimed they had found their real home at last, in Paris most frequently. But I seldom believed them. Most of them were like myself, wandering around restlessly, looking for something that couldn't be found, always homesick. I remember how homesick I was for New York my first trip abroad. And yet I had there almost nothing to be homesick for, almost no friends, no home except for a cheap hotel.

"The colonial Englishman is another homesick creature, but I think he is homesick for the land his race has tilled for generations. We, abroad, are homesick for something less tangible. I have felt as if I had come home in America when, lying in an upper berth in a Pullman, unable to see, I have heard a voice speaking in familiar accents on a station platform. Part of the American homesickness abroad is probably due to the longing for a sensation of space which cannot be satisfied in Europe. Beautiful little England seems stuffy, overcultivated, overpopulated to the American.

"We are still pioneers, that is why we are restless. That is perhaps why we have not yet created great art and literature. I believe in America. To me she is magnificent. When we are ready we shall have a great literature—indeed I think we are already on our way to achieving it. I think American writers are doing more interesting work nowadays than English authors. I find that the English themselves are often ready to believe it.

"For myself I feel as if now at last I were through wandering. In my last trip abroad I felt as if I had had enough. Over in Brooklyn in the cheap little boarding house where I live I am perfectly content. I come into New York not oftener than once a week and when I do it is like a holiday. I see it for the fabulous city it is. I am working hard and completely happy in my work. Even in the heat I feel no need to stop, and that makes me happy, for I hate heat, and it seems to me that the fact that I can work in it proves that I am working well. Perhaps my finding myself in my writing accounts for the end of my restlessness.

"I have become systematic in my methods of writing. For years I wrote without system on loose sheets of paper, much of which I lost, but reams of which I have stored in trunks. It seemed that I had the energy to conceive and complete a work, but never the power to get it off to a publisher. Indeed, as I was often losing important parts of it, it was sometimes quite out of the question to do so.

"Then a friend persuaded me to write in canvas-covered ledgers so that my work would not be scattered. In that way I wrote *Look Homeward, Angel*. Following the friend's advice I set myself to a schedule of so much work to be completed a day and hold myself to it. I can keep up a pace of about five hours a day. With less I accomplish too little, with more I get exhausted.

"The first novel, as I have said, was in a sense—but not literally—autobiographical. I believe that is the common way for young writers to begin. The objective viewpoint comes with maturity and experience. *October Fair* I feel is more objectively conceived, and yet very intimately personal. To tell you its substance would be impossible. But it is very long and divided into four parts and has a very definite form.

"For that matter I feel that *Look Homeward, Angel* is not so formless as its critics said. I don't feel that it is even a long novel when you consider its substance. Recently I read a French novel which had been praised for the perfection of its form and its compactness. The whole story concerned a love affair which didn't come off. The entire first chapter of this novel of a little more than 200 pages was devoted to an account of a walk in the woods at which nothing special happened. Do you call that compactness and brevity? I think that with all my hundreds of pages I was more brief.

"I like long novels. Lately the enthusiasm of a friend has started me to reading the great Russians. I have just found Tolstoy's *War and Peace.*

"There are some books that I read all the time. They include the Bible, John Donne, and especially Shakespeare. It seems to me that Shakespeare in his vast understanding of humanity was a sort of god. I imagine that he was one with this insatiable capacity to live. By that I don't mean that he wanted long life, but simply that while life was with him he demanded that it be full.

"Also lately I have been getting acquainted with some of the authors my reviewers have accused me of imitating. I'm afraid that I took my reviews too seriously, but in some instances I have reason to be glad of it. One reviewer, whose identity I have forgotten, compared me to Whitman. I had no rest until I had sought out his works, which were largely unfamiliar to me, and had digested them. He was a wonderful discovery. It seems to me that he is one of the most American of American writers. Many of his ideas now seem out of date, such as his enthusiasm for democracy, an impossible ideal to my mind, yet essentially he is the real American."

I had kept Mr. Wolfe talking a long time on an exceptionally uncomfortable afternoon. He had lighted cigarette after cigarette as he talked, had wiped beads of perspiration from his forehead. It was high time to let him go. But I had been on his trail for more than a year and couldn't let him go with any questions unasked. I pulled forth a list of notes I had made in reading *Look Homeward, Angel.* Gravely he inspected it with me, and to my astonishment found quite clear and intelligible such cryptic notations as "the fabulous" and "ultimate ambition."

"Yes, the fabulous—all life is that," said he. "Life is greater than ourselves. It seems as if our poor senses were never qualified fully to receive any experience. The fables of the ancients have powerfully influenced my imagination. I have named one section of *October Fair* for the opponent of Hercules—Antaeus.

"For the ultimate ambition, I want to write about fifteen novels, all long ones, and to get somehow an assured income of about $200 a month. If I could have that and with it the freedom to write all the time, I'd be perfectly happy."

Miss Starkey wrote, in a letter to Richard Walser, July 31, 1982, "I never took notes on this sort of interview—as opposed to news stories where it was necessary to record facts—but relied on my memory, then very good, since my Transcript *stories always pleased. Once I was curious enough to consult my diary on the date of the interview and found only a reference to him as a 'shy giant.'" She said that, though she never saw Wolfe again, there were two other contacts: "One was an enthusiastic postcard from an island in Maine which I had recommended for a vacation. Another was a phone call when he was in Boston, staying at the old Hotel Bellevue. He asked me to join him for an evening, but alas I was on my way out to a prior engagement. Since he was staying over I wonder that neither of us suggested a meeting the following day; anyway we didn't." She commented in a letter to Aldo Magi, August 28, 1982, that "a social date with what I called my 'shy giant' might have been beyond my capacity."*

Among Starkey's many books is The Devil in Massachusetts *(1949), a story of the Salem witchcraft hysteria. Besides her work with newspapers, for many years she taught college English in Virginia and Connecticut.*

New York *Herald Tribune*, February 18, 1935

The first months of 1935 were a busy and anxious time for Wolfe. So uncertain and nervous was he about the reception of Of Time and the River that he decided to flee the local scene for Paris before its publication. See The Letters of Thomas Wolfe to His Mother *(Chapel Hill, 1968), 244–45.*

Scribner's had every reason to expect a tremendous success and, as a promotional tactic, set up an interview for Wolfe with the influential New York Herald Tribune *on Sunday, February 17. It turned out to be his most unhappy encounter with the public press. According to Elizabeth Nowell in* Thomas Wolfe *(Garden City, N.Y., 1960), 248–49, 301, the jittery novelist had, as might have been expected, "forgotten all about the visit of the interviewer, Sanderson Vanderbilt, till the time when he was scheduled to arrive, and had then rushed out to eat lunch and buy a bottle of liquor with which to fortify himself for the ordeal, leaving a note for Vanderbilt to walk into his apartment and 'make himself at home.'"*

Vanderbilt proceeded to do just that. During the hour before Wolfe returned, the reporter jotted down minute details of the writer's untidy housekeeping, inspected his mutilated lamp and eccentric alarm clock, and read whatever papers were lying about. Finally Wolfe made his appearance, and the journalist recorded for print all the excitable novelist's casual and off-the-record remarks. When attempting to explain the difficult role of the artist in America, Wolfe stammered, "H-h-here! T-t-take this! I've s-said it all in here m-much better than I can express it to you now." Vanderbilt speedily pocketed the only copy of the first draft of what would become The Story of a Novel.

The article was titled "Thomas Wolfe Cuts 2d Book to 450,000 Words—Author of 'Look Homeward, Angel' Weary Pruning 'Of Time and the River'—Expects to Do 5 Million—Finds It Hard to Write in America, So He's Leaving" and appeared with a photograph by Jerome Zerbe.

With a good two inches of blue shirt separating the bottom of his rumpled vest from the top of his unpressed pants, Thomas Wolfe, thirty-four-year-old novelist whose *Look Homeward, Angel* made him a white hope of America's leading critics four years ago, barged into his apartment at 5 Montague Terrace, Brooklyn, yesterday afternoon.

The literary gentleman, who is six feet five inches tall, stalked about the place bemoaning that he was not only a good hour late for an interview, but that his next novel *Of Time and the River*, to be issued on March 8, has been cut from 700,000 to a mere 450,000 words. It will be the second of a series of six novels planned by Mr. Wolfe, who expects to write 5,000,000 words and then sorrowfully see them pruned down to a scant 2,000,000.

Mr. Wolfe had promised to meet a reporter at 2 o'clock, but the thought of an interview so terrified him that he fled to a restaurant for luncheon. The result was that it was not until 3 that he felt sufficiently fortified to face a camera and questioner. Scrawled in the handwriting with which he turns out his bales of manuscripts was a note stuck in his letter box. It read:

"Have gone out to lunch but will be back in few minutes. If you get no answer when you ring my bell, ring superintendent's bell and she will take you up to my place. Make yourself at home until I get back. T. WOLFE."

Mr. Wolfe's "place" turned out to be on the fourth floor of a five-story brownstone house in Brooklyn Heights—one which formerly commanded a view of the harbor, but which now has become simply dismal, what with larger apartments that have been built between it and the water. In the creaky old building the author has two rooms for which he pays $45 a month and considers it a bargain.

An icebox stood in the bathroom, but it evidently was not used, for Mr. Wolfe had placed a bottle of milk, half a dozen eggs, and some sliced bacon out on the window sill. There was a bridge lamp in the corner, but it lacked both shade and bulbs. A telephone on the mantel proved simply an ornament and near by rested an unpaid $17.18 bill for its services.

The bed in the adjoining room had been hastily made and beside it was an old green alarm clock that operates only when flat on its face. In the room's lone bookshelf were such volumes as Tolstoy's *Anna*

Karenina, several of the de la Roche *Jalna* series, *Cakes and Ale* by
Maugham, a Manhattan telephone directory, *Ulysses* by James Joyce,
yellow paper-backed French novels, and several copies of *Look Homeward, Angel*.

A clay jug was filled with stubs of pencils with which Mr. Wolfe
writes. On the table lay a first edition of *Of Time and the River*,
which he had corrected and which showed that typists and linotype
men have their troubles in deciphering the author's jerky script.
"Elemental," for example, had been printed instead of "eternal." Mr.
Wolfe had had to change "numerous" to "murmurous"; "moist" had
been corrected to read "most"; and the compositor had read "sweet"
where Mr. Wolfe had written "secret."

Downstairs a taxicab door slammed and presently Mr. Wolfe burst
into the room, penitent for his tardiness and dusting cigarette ashes
off his trousers. "Gosh," he exclaimed, "I'm sorry I kept you waiting." Then he settled down to discuss his writing. There will be six
novels in all, he said, and in them he will attempt to trace the development of 150 years in America. *Look Homeward, Angel* deals with
the years from 1884 to 1920; *Of Time and the River* with 1920 to 1925;
The October Fair will cover from 1925 to 1928; and *The Hills beyond
Pentland* from 1838 to 1926. Mr. Wolfe still has to write *The Death of
the Enemy*, which will carry the theme from 1928 to 1933, and *Pacific End* from 1791 to 1884.

"I hope the whole thing will be kind of like a plant," said Mr.
Wolfe, stretching his bulk out in a rickety chair and clutching at his
sparse black hair. "Now don't make that sound kind of fancy. Sort of
like a plant that's had a lot of roots in it. I guess the general plan back
of these books is the story of a man's looking for his father. Everybody in the world—not only men but women—is looking for a father.
Looking for some person of superior strength. Some person outside
of themselves to whom they can attach their belief."

Over and over again Mr. Wolfe, who was born in Asheville, N.C.,
the son of a stonecutter, cried out vehemently that he was "born of
working people." He declared: "It's hard to write things in America,
and that's why it's good to do so when you succeed. We've got a new

language here—we can't talk like Matthew Arnold or James Russell Lowell; he's an American, of course, but he's trying to talk like an Englishman."

Mr. Wolfe was graduated from the University of North Carolina in 1920 and then received an M.A. degree from Harvard. He wrote his *Look Homeward, Angel* in 1930 in Switzerland and then came to Brooklyn to work at night on his second novel, sleep by day, and prowl about the borough during his hours of recreation. He is a restive bachelor.

"I thought Brooklyn was a good place to come to work," he said, staring about the disordered room with piercing black eyes. "And I've worked my head off here. But I'm going away now, at the end of this month. Yes, going away on a freight boat—to Italy, to Spain, to France, and I hope I'll get to Egypt. And I'm going as a tourist. When I see a sightseeing bus, I'm going to hop it.

"I've been learning about writing like hell in the last four years. You might say I've worked like hell. I've got to write 5,000,000 words, but you fix it up if it sounds like boasting because, damn it, I need some money and I want to sell this book."

Mr. Wolfe said that when he started on his first novel he thought he would be able to express the entire idea in some 250,000 words, but now it has stretched well into the millions. The book swelled up within him, he said, "like a raincloud." He had always wanted to be a writer but considered that aspiration "a sort of romantic dream." His mother, he chuckled, still sends him clippings of authors who have made good. She adds as a postscript to her son, "You can be a writer, too."

"I wrote on death and love," he rambled on. "I wrote of the way it is to wake up in the morning in this country, and of riding in a Pullman train with a good-looking woman opposite you, and of getting off the Fall River boat."

All of Mr. Wolfe's writing is done with a lead pencil and he gets stenographers to type his work. The side of the room was piled high with manuscripts. He writes in ledgers, notebooks, and on copy paper.

"I haven't done any work at all during the last three or four months and I feel like a bum," said Mr. Wolfe, getting up and striding about the room. "When you finish a book it's the worst time in the world. You hope you get famous and make some money. But you got too close to the book while you were writing it and you forget it when you're through. You can't believe you're guilty."

"Sunday," he said, suddenly, peering out of the window into the twilight. "Wouldn't you know it's Sunday just to look out at that queer light. I've hated Brooklyn—cursed it more times—I've wandered at night all over this rusty jungle to which I came because I thought I'd be able to write here. But I think I'm going to have an affection for the place when I leave. I've seen the damndest things out here in Brooklyn. It's a great, brutal mass. Manhattan has some integrity, but this place is a great, formless, huge, enormous blot, and 3,000,000 people live here. All the underdogs in the world live here. The dishwashers, the fellers who run the subway trains, the fellers in cafeterias, the elevator operators, the scrubwomen, the fellers who work in chain grocery stores—they all live here. But it's a great place, too. I've seen stuff out here in great uncharted places that nobody in New York ever heard of."

Mr. Wolfe lit another cigarette and ran his fingers wildly through his hair.

"I'm a nut," he cried.

Next morning when he read the interview, Wolfe was consumed with rage. For days he ranted that the despicable Vanderbilt had sold him out, had repaid his sincerity and trust with abuse. When the interview was reprinted later in the Asheville Citizen, *Wolfe's anger knew no bounds: he had been ridiculed and treated with contempt before his own home folks.*

Wolfe knew how to take revenge on those who displeased him—not with sticks and stones but with words. In A Note on Experts: Dexter Vespasian Joyner *(New York, 1939), he avouched with unforgotten bitterness that "newspapermen are whores," though some were not so bad as others. But for the worst of them, he wrote, "Give me the good old homely, ink-stained harlot of the city room, the plain old whore of daily print. Give me the fellow who will come to see you for an interview, who will read your mail when you've gone out to get a drink for him, who will look at your telephone bill to see how much you owe, who will try the telephone to see if the service has been cut off, who will poke around in dusty corners, investigate your dirty linen, take advantage of your youth, your excitement, your enthusiasm, your eagerness to make a good impression and have a good piece in the paper and will twist it all around, garble it all, mangle it all, make a fool of you, betray your honesty and your youth, betray the innocence and belief of man, all for the purpose of 'getting a good story' out of it. Give me this kind of whore, I say, because you know just where you stand with him, and in the end you won't be fooled."* Wolfe's strictures are devastating, of course, and there is no doubt whom he has in mind.

Sanderson Vanderbilt, a graduate of Amherst, left the Herald Tribune in 1938 and joined the staff of the New Yorker magazine, where he was a writer and editor for the next thirty years.

Dagens Nyheder, June 18, 1935

In Paris, Wolfe received word from Maxwell Perkins that Of Time and the River *had received glowing reviews. He then went on to England and Holland before arriving in Berlin on May 7, where he "awoke to find himself famous."* Look Homeward, Angel, *in its excellent German translation, was already greatly admired there, and now came reports from New York about* Of Time and the River. *For over a month Wolfe was enthusiastically greeted everywhere in the city, recognized by passers-by on the streets, acclaimed by the German literati, and entertained lavishly at the American embassy. But eventually the excitement and intemperate high living took their toll, and Wolfe retreated to Copenhagen to recuperate. So exhausted was he that he had to seek the help of a physician.*

Shortly after his arrival, editor C. H. Clemmensen of the Dagens Nyheder (Daily News) *and its literary reporter Hakon Stangerup called on Wolfe at his hotel. At that time many Danish newspapermen chose not to use direct quotations in interviews, giving them the appearance of feature stories. "Lynskud ved Hr. Nat-og-Dag" (Flash by Mr. Night-and-Day) appeared in the* Dagens Nyheder *on June 18, 1935. A few obvious errors, such as that his portable typewriter was a gift from Berlin friends and that he himself took the manuscript of* Look Homeward, Angel *to Scribner's, are left uncorrected, though it is not impossible that Wolfe was responsible for the misstatements. See Richard S. Kennedy and Paschal Reeves (eds.),* The Notebooks of Thomas Wolfe *(Chapel Hill, 1970), 749, 756.*

With the interview was a photograph captioned "Thomas Wolfe, the successful American author. He hesitantly gave me this photo, taken in Berlin, saying, 'Tell your readers that in reality I don't look like a man who just got out of jail.'" On his return to New York, Wolfe presented a copy of the photograph to Belinda Jelliffe, who, incidentally, was the donor of the typewriter. See Elizabeth Nowell (ed.), The Letters of Thomas Wolfe *(New York, 1956), frontispiece and p. 433.*

Quite unnoticed and unmentioned, one of America's most discussed new novelists has been in Copenhagen for the last couple of days. Let me introduce you to thirty-four-year-old Thomas Wolfe, a young, broad-shouldered giant with coal black hair and pensive eyes, the author of *Of Time and the River*, number-two bestseller at the moment in the United States, a man on the way to great world renown, the new Sinclair Lewis.

I spent some time with Wolfe yesterday. He told me how he had come up here from Berlin, where he had visited good friends for a couple of weeks and had a wonderful time. Now he had traveled to Copenhagen just to rest for a couple of days in a big city where not a soul knew him, and where he was sure to be able to walk about unnoticed. Tomorrow he is going to Bremen for his return to New York.

He really succeeded in having a few undisturbed days in this town, as he had planned. That nobody noticed him proves what I have always maintained—that Copenhagen is one of the easiest cities for a famous foreigner to hide in—much easier, for instance, than London or New York. The reason probably lies in the different ways that Danish and English or American reporters operate.

Do you know that on a fall day in 1918, at a time when all of Germany was in flames following the big collapse after the war, one of Germany's most discussed men, namely no one less than General Erich Ludendorff, sat cozily for several consecutive evenings at Hammers Fiskerestaurant, G1. Strand 34, and ate his dinner without a single newspaper discovering him? As a journalist, I have always felt ashamed over this fact—that not a single one of us found him and set up a world-historic interview with him.

But now, Thomas Wolfe. He is a big sad boy, quite unspoiled by the sudden world success which has fallen upon him with his last book. He is somewhat of a phenomenon of an American author. Although he cannot use a typewriter, his friends in Berlin had presented him with a nice little portable. It was standing in a corner of his hotel room, and once in a while he would give it a mean look. He was convinced that he would never make friends with it.

He told me, however, that ever since he was fifteen years old, he had been unable to get near a pencil and paper without immediately picking them up and starting to write, at times almost in ecstasy.

His problem was—and still is, he confesses—the perfectly fantastic number of words that come to him as soon as he sits down. Condensation is lacking. He can write only giant books, and he feels unable to cut the once-written manuscripts. A very good friend of his, who is employed by Scribner's in New York, has done the editing of his books.

About his beginnings: born in Asheville, North Carolina, son of a stonecutter whose specialty was tombstones, college-educated, then to New York as a teacher of English at one of the big universities, small salary, wrote every night in his Spartan quarters, wrote and wrote, felt convinced that his book would be so good that no publisher could refuse to undertake it. But when the manuscript was finally finished one day, it was a pile of closely written pages which reached almost from the floor to the ceiling. His courage waned. He took the whole stack to Scribner's and was given to understand that under no circumstances could a gigantic novel like that be published. He traveled to Europe. Ending up one day in Vienna with two dollars in his pocket, he got a telegram from New York: negotiations with him were desired about the publication of his book.

He managed to get the means for a hasty return home. Visiting the publisher, he found that they wished to publish the book in abbreviated form. The friend in New York promised to help. He left half an hour later with five hundred dollars in his pocket, just a meager advance on the fortune that he was going to make. That was in 1929.

The book that was published somewhat later was *Look Homeward, Angel*, which sold 15,000 copies. Not bad for a first book, but nothing in comparison to the sales of his second book *Of Time and the River*.

Both are about 1,000 pages long. In spite of energetic attempts to shorten them, Thomas Wolfe tells me that it is his plan to write four more books similar to the two already published, a gigantic work depicting one hundred and fifty years of American history, an American cavalcade with about 2,000 different characters. He figures that he will have the work finished in five years. He has all of it inside him, he says, beating his broad chest with his fist; and he simply cannot help writing it. If only he could learn to write in a more condensed manner—but there is a compulsion to write, without self-imposed limitations.

He is now about to be translated into many languages. When Sinclair Lewis was in Stockholm a couple of years ago to receive the Nobel Prize, he mentioned Wolfe in his acceptance speech as "the coming man." At that time the greatly successful *Of Time and the River* had not yet been published. Few American critics now doubt that Lewis was right.

His native town of Asheville was very upset over his first book because it thought that it could find portraits of all the town's well-known personalities in it. Asheville is a town of 40,000 inhabitants. Thomas Wolfe is inclined to believe that all 40,000 have read the novel. Several of the residents have threatened in letters to murder him if he ever sets foot there again.

He considers himself innocently persecuted. Naturally he has written from his own experiences (what author has done otherwise?), but he maintains absolutely that he had no intention of portraying either this or that particular person. *Look Homeward, Angel* is generally viewed as an expression of the longing for a father—which, Wolfe feels, all modern young people have.

The translation of this interview from the Danish was made by Ruth Shaw of Memphis, Tennessee.

New York *Times,* July 5, 1935

After four months in Europe, Wolfe returned to New York. In Germany the translation of Look Homeward, Angel *had been so successful that he was looked upon as the great new American writer. His triumphant welcome in Berlin brought him the fame for which he had long wished. And now in America, with* Of Time and the River *on all best-seller lists, his name was everywhere familiar and honored. When the* Bremen *docked on the Fourth of July, reporters from the newspapers were at the pier. The following article appeared under the title "Brevity to Be Goal of Thomas Wolfe—Author, Back from European Tour, Admits He 'Writes Too Much of Everything'—Promises He'll 'Learn'—Has Faith in Our Literature and Says His Next Novel Will Be about New York."*

Thomas Wolfe, called by critics one of the most promising young novelists of the day since his *Look Homeward, Angel* and *Of Time and the River* attracted wide attention, returned yesterday on the North German Lloyd liner *Bremen* after a four-month tour of England, France, Germany, and Scandinavia.

A gargantuan writer of gargantuan novels (his last book was shaved down to 450,000 words after considerable brain-cudgeling), the 34-year-old author came back home with a promise to literary reviewers who have looked forward with mingled joy and dread to the four novels yet to come in his series of six. They have accused him of a dislike of brevity.

"I know I write too much of everything," he said. "The thing I am going to learn some day is that you might write one of the best things you ever put on paper, but it doesn't necessarily belong in the book at hand. I am going to learn, though. I'll work hard and I know I can do it."

Several inches taller than six feet, and proportionately broad, Mr. Wolfe came down a corridor of the liner to the foyer where inter-

viewers were waiting for him, warm and nervous. He began by trying to talk reporters out of the interview but before the afternoon
had ended and the *Bremen* had passed up the harbor to her West
Forty-sixth Street pier, he had described his trip through Europe
and outlined his plans for the future.

"I guess I'll be feeling pretty guilty about all this talking by
tonight," he said, with a wry smile. "So please don't have me saying
anything silly."

"You know," he said, "I haven't read all the criticism of my book
yet, but honestly I think I've got more sense of form than they think
I have. How can you lay down such cut-and-dried forms for a novel
when there are so many great ones as far apart as James Joyce and
Jane Austen?"

He was amazed to learn in Germany that writers and publishers
there consider contemporary American literature "the most interesting, the most vital and original writing in the world." Mr. Wolfe,
too, has great faith in the modern American literature, and when he
was asked if he was greatly influenced by James Joyce as in his first
novel, he replied: "No more."

"I think," he added, "we have our own literature. Honestly, in the
next twenty years we are going to turn out some grand books. America has never really been written about. There is so much for American writers yet to do. So far, I think the man who has best described
America to me was Walt Whitman."

Mr. Wolfe said he would look for a small apartment in Manhattan
and go to work on his next book. It will be about New York and he
wants to know more about the city before finishing it, so he will not
go back to Brooklyn, which has been his home for five years.

*Greater than the pleasure of being surrounded by reporters was Wolfe's
happiness at being met at the dock by his editor, Maxwell Perkins of
Scribner's. First, they had lunch at a restaurant floating on an East
River barge, then leisurely dropped by a number of bars Wolfe had fre-
quented in the past. In Brooklyn at sunset they gazed down from the*

roof of the Prince George Hotel at the magnificence of the harbor and the city. Their feverish drinking and talking went on until long past midnight.

It was the most exultant day in all of Wolfe's life, the day about which he reminded Perkins from a Seattle hospital in the last letter he was ever to write: "I shall always think of you and feel about you the way it was that Fourth of July three years ago when you met me at the boat, and we went out on the cafe on the river and had a drink and later went on top of the tall building, and all the strangeness and the glory and the power of life and of the city was below." See Elizabeth Nowell, Thomas Wolfe *(Garden City, N.Y., 1960), 279–282.*

Rocky Mountain News, August 8, 1935

One result of Wolfe's newly found fame was an invitation to participate in the annual Writers' Conference at the University of Colorado from July 22 to August 9, 1935. Usually declining requests to talk before formal gatherings, he was excited about this invitation because it would give him a chance to see a part of the country that was new to him. On August 6 he spoke for an hour and forty minutes. The talk, which he called "The Making of a Novel," was an intense confession of his feelings about producing his second novel. The audience was quickly captivated by the young novelist and what he had to say, and most observers agreed that Wolfe unquestionably was the "hit" of the conference. Two days later an interview titled "Write Hard and at Home, Advises Author at C.U.," datelined Boulder "By Associated Press," appeared in the Rocky Mountain News *(Denver). More than likely it was the work of Thomas Hornsby Ferril, poet and journalist, who on July 31 had been with Wolfe and others on a panel discussion titled "Poetry and Intelligibility." Following the conference, Ferril drove Wolfe through the surrounding mountains for several days.*

If you want to write, start writing now in your own home town and write every day as hard as you can; do not think you have to go to Paris and wait for inspiration to strike.

That is the advice of Thomas Wolfe, young American author of *Look Homeward, Angel* and *Of Time and the River*, who visited the Rocky Mountain Writers Conference at the University of Colorado Wednesday.

"People who go to Paris or Italy to do a little writing," he said, "are only trying to get away from themselves and their own laziness. The place to write is in Boulder or Greeley or Denver or Timbuctoo, or wherever you happen to live."

He scorned the belief that a writer must wait for inspiration. "If you sit around thinking inspiration will come the 13th of every February or so, you'll never get any writing done. You are a literary workman, and ought to work every day."

Describing how his own novels were written, Wolfe told of the torture and anguish an author feels in starting work.

"You have an awful, hollow, ghastly feeling, wondering whether you can write what you want to write or not. Then as my book began to grow before me, a wild sense of exultation and joyous elation seized me. There seemed to be a thundercloud pregnant with life within me; suddenly the thunder came and the cloud burst and it began to rain, and it's been raining ever since."

His first novel, *Look Homeward, Angel*, was written in 1930 [actually Wolfe began writing the novel in England the summer of 1926 and completed the manuscript in New York in March, 1928] when he was studying abroad under the Guggenheim scholarship for creative writing. Since it was written, he has received the Scribner's prize for a long short story, and has written over two million words in stories and material for new novels.

Wolfe was born in Asheville, N.C., was graduated from the state university there, and in 1923 received his M.A. degree from Harvard University.

He urges writers to study their own country and write about what they know best. "The process of discovering our America is the most difficult but most magnificent task that lies before us," he said.

Boulder *Daily Camera*, August 12, 1935

Wolfe's evaluation of the Writers' Conference at the University of Colorado was expressed to Forrest Crossen in a report entitled "Future of Writers Conference Discussed by Faculty Members."

"I have never attended a writers' conference before. Frankly I was a little troubled about coming out here—not only because I'm not a platform speaker, with no experience in public speaking, but I didn't know what I was going to run into, whether the atmosphere would be stiff and academic or not.

"I found that this feeling is utterly groundless. This group is not only friendly and hospitable but immensely intelligent. I have been astonished at the superb quality of the lectures and at the high level of effort and aspiration which it seems to me has marked the whole proceeding.

"Frankly, I was dubious about the whole purpose and value of a writers' conference before I came here, but I no longer have any doubt that a work of tremendous importance can be achieved here and that many young writers of talent are going to derive the lasting benefit from these meetings.

"I may never return here as a speaker, since public speaking is not in my line and a great labor of writing to which the next years of my life must be devoted lies before me, but I hope to return as a witness and spectator to a work in which I am proud to think I have played some small part and whose future growth I shall look forward to with the most confident interest and belief.

"Finally, I should like to say that I came here a somewhat perturbed and worried stranger, not knowing exactly what to expect or what I would run into and all of you have made me a friend.

Reprinted by permission of the *Daily Camera*.

"It is therefore with genuine regret and a little sadness that I see the conference come to its close and the hour of my own departure near. I cannot conclude this statement without paying a final tribute of thanks not only to all the people of the University and Boulder who have made my visit here so pleasing and so memorable but also to the fine talents, distinguished abilities and high earnestness of my colleagues, Mr. Edward Davison, program director of the Conference; Mr. Robert Frost, Mr. Robert Penn Warren, Miss Martha Foley, Mr. Whit Burnett, Blanche Young McNeal and Mignon Baker, who have worked together in a spirit of perfect harmony and fine enthusiasm to present what seems to me to be the most extraordinary and instructive series of lectures, talks and conferences I have ever listened to."

Forrest Crossen, a Boulder resident since 1923, has spent his life talking to railroaders, cattlemen, cavalry officers, and frontiersmen. His first profiles were published in the Boulder Daily Camera *in a column called "People I Meet." Best known for his "Western Yesterdays" books, Crossen's latest book,* The Golden Mirage *(Fort Collins, Colo., 1982) is a historical novel about Coronado's search for the Seven Cities of Cibola.*

Berlin, 1935
Courtesy North Carolina Collection, University of North Carolina Library, Chapel Hill

With Thomas Hornsby Ferril, Boulder, Colorado, August, 1935
Courtesy Thomas Wolfe Collection, Pack Memorial Public Library, Asheville, North
Carolina

Frank Wolfe, Mrs. Julia Wolfe, Thomas Wolfe, Effie Wolfe Gambrell, Fred Wolfe,
Mabel Wolfe Wheaton, Asheville, Summer, 1937
Courtesy Thomas Wolfe Collection, Pack Memorial Public Library, Asheville, North
Carolina

During a newspaper interview, Denver, May, 1938
Courtesy Thomas Wolfe Collection, Pack Memorial Public Library, Asheville, North Carolina

Wolfe with traveling companions T. Raymond Conway and Edward M. Miller,
Glacier National Park, June, 1938
Courtesy North Carolina Collection, University of North Carolina Library, Chapel Hill

Guests at the Haglund home: Theodore Abrahams, Mrs. Margaret Haglund,
Ivar Haglund, Thomas Wolfe, Mrs. Theresa Stevens, Mrs. Erma Butler, "Turk"
Tergis, and James Stevens, Seattle, July 4, 1938
Courtesy North Carolina Collection, University of North Carolina Library, Chapel Hill

An uncast bust of Thomas Wolfe by Nat Werner
Courtesy North Carolina Collection, University of North Carolina Library, Chapel Hill

With James Stevens, Seattle, June 17, 1938
Courtesy Seattle *Post-Intelligencer*

St. Louis *Star-Times*, September 20, 1935

Wolfe visited St. Louis on returning from his trip west to speak at the Writers' Conference at the University of Colorado, with further stopover visits in Hollywood, San Francisco, Reno, and Salt Lake City. "From the outset of his trip, he had planned to look up the place where Julia Wolfe had operated the 'North Carolina' boarding house during the St. Louis Fair in 1904. Now, in mid-September, he was there to bring back the moments of a past self three years old in the house where his brother Grover died. The visit to the site, like all returns to places long left behind, overwhelmed him with the strangeness of familiarity in the midst of change. The emotional impact of this experience began a seething which boiled over two years later when Wolfe wrote 'The Lost Boy,' his most intense treatment of the search for lost time." See Richard S. Kennedy, The Literary Career of Thomas Wolfe: The Window of Memory *(Chapel Hill, 1962), 290.*

While in St. Louis Wolfe was interviewed by a staff reporter from the Star-Times. *The interview was titled "Thomas Wolfe Visits City—Says He'll Write a 'Really Great' Book—Author of Best-Seller Now Busy Putting on Paper Life He Observes—'Technique Can Come Later.'"*

Thomas Wolfe, whose novel *Of Time and the River* has been on the best-seller lists for months and has been held by many to be the most significant work of fiction to be published this year, stopped over for a day and a night here this week on his return to New York from the west.

While in St. Louis the author visited the house near Cates and Academy avenues in which he lived during the "World's Fair" here. Wolfe remembered the house very well, although he had not seen it since he was 3 years old and the name of the avenue had been changed without his knowledge from Fairmount to Cates.

He related that he spoke to the woman now living in the house, and in a moment of forgetfulness pointed out that his brother had died in that room "right there." Later he was so ashamed for having startled her, he said, that he did not wish to reveal the exact address.

Wolfe reported he had practically wasted the summer "loafing around." The only work he had done, he said, was "a piddling 100,000 or 200,000 words of notes." His last novel ran to something like 450,000 words. His remark was made with the utmost candor, and anyone who had heard him make it would have sworn he was filled with remorse over being so lazy.

It would take Wolfe himself to describe himself adequately. Six feet 6 inches "or maybe a little more" in height; broad at the shoulders and rotund at the waist, he is an astonishingly big fellow. To talk with him while he stands beside one is decidedly uncomfortable, he dwarfs his companion so completely.

It is not, however, his size that is most impressive about him. It is the fact that he is continually in what writers term a fine frenzy. He is so intensely alive: so curious about everything: so keenly aware, as to make those about him seem pallid and phlegmatic.

He seems uncomfortable if he is not talking when in the presence of others. Words stream from him as though he were impatient of having to use them to transmit his thought. He stutters a bit in the urgency to say a lot quickly.

Almost anyone else who talked so much would be thought a boor. Yet Wolfe never seems to be monopolizing the conversation. His simplest statement strikes the hearer as being a profound personal revelation.

Despite his dominating presence and the deference that is paid him, he never speaks in a didactic manner. He makes no pretensions to great wisdom. He is simply without inhibitions. He likes people and he likes living; he feels a desperate need to express those likings, and it happens that his expression of them is vivid and stimulating.

While he was a guest at the home of J. Lesser Goldman, Oak Knoll, Clayton, Wolfe leaned forward on a small bench in the midst of a dozen or so persons and made all these traits manifest. In shirt-sleeves, his bulky trousers upheld by galluses which could safely be used to tie up a fair-sized man; his black hair roached back but resisting the process; his rather Indian-like features sharp and his face never at rest, Wolfe talked of writing.

"I know I don't know anything about writing," he said. "I'm bewildered. But I'm going to know how to write before I get through. My father was a stonecutter and a darned good one. That was his trade. I'm going to be as good at my trade as he was at his.

"I'm not worrying about technique now. I'm of the opinion that I have a pretty prodigious talent, but I'm not concerned yet with developing a finished aesthetic. There are too many things that I want to get down on paper. I want to put down everything I've observed about life. Technique can come later.

"It seems to me that a novelist's first business is to report life accurately. I haven't much patience with the writers who become wonderful craftsmen but never have anything to say.

"For the first time in my life I've gotten some celebrity and a bit of money. It would be silly to say I don't enjoy it. I like it so much that I'm going to work all the harder, and get more money and more celebrity.

"I'm in love with America and I think it's important to portray Americans—how they feel when a freight train goes by, and the rest. There is such a thing as a distinctive American culture. It's a coat of many colors, but still it's a coat. It's not simply an amalgam of European traditions."

Wolfe remarked that he had become "suspicious of those birds—reporters," since his return from abroad a few months ago. "I gave them a long spiel on the future of American writing," he said, "and all they used in their stories was a trifling little anecdote I had told them."

The anecdote had to do with Wolfe's inability to ruffle—with strong drink—the composure of an English servant. Wolfe said he was rather nettled by the ensuing crop of letters, particularly from women of the Middle West, applauding the servant and berating him for his "filthy" book.

"Whatever else *Of Time and the River* is," said Wolfe, "it is certainly not filth."

The 34-year-old author said that since critics had complained that the novel was autobiographical, readers had outdone themselves remembering exactly when and where certain events in the book had actually taken place. "Episodes which were wholly imaginary," he said, "have actually gotten me into trouble through people thinking they remembered them."

"I'm aware," he added, "that the autobiographical element has been overworked in my works, and that all the really great books have been highly original. I'll write a really great, highly original book some day."

When he does, it is certain to be American to the core. He is enthusiastic about every section of the country. He was especially enthusiastic about the West, which he had not seen before his recent trip, that is, all of it "except—possibly—Hollywood."

Originally from North Carolina, student at Harvard, resident of Brooklyn for five years, Wolfe had found that all Americans were "real people—like North Carolinians," and all very specially American, "with the possible exception of sophisticated society in New York."

For the most part, Wolfe illustrates in his person the qualities of his prose—its soaring, leaping, untrammeled aliveness, its lushness of imagery and phrases, its prolixity and formlessness and excitement and continual wonder. There is, however, a difference. There is no apparent flair for comedy in Wolfe the author. It was, therefore, a surprise to find him in person always aware of the comical aspect of things.

He told a great many anecdotes but one may be singled out. He had been afraid to meet Dorothy Parker—"she was supposed to be poisonous, you know"—and upon meeting her, he related, he told her he was frightened, having heard of her making such scathing remarks. With a naivete equal to Wolfe's own, she replied, very earnestly and very innocently, "They do say the most AWFUL things about me, Mr. Wolfe."

For the "trifling little anecdote" about the snobbishness and "composure of an English servant," see "English Butler Ruffles Calm of Thomas Wolfe—Author, Back Home, Finds Ruggles Snobbery Eclipsed," New York Herald Tribune, *July 5, 1935;* Time, *July 15, 1935, p. 45; and Elizabeth Nowell,* Thomas Wolfe *(Garden City, N.Y., 1960), 265–66.*

The staff reporter who conducted this interview was Reed Hynds.

Portland *Morning Oregonian*, October 18, 1935

With Wolfe's intense genealogical interest in the Westall branch of his family that had settled in the West, it is not difficult to imagine his willingness, if not delight, to talk with David W. Hazen of the Portland Oregonian, *who was in New York and asked to interview him. The interview, titled "Author to End Series in Oregon—Thomas Wolfe's Relatives Live Near Eugene," was datelined New York, October 17.*

Thomas Wolfe, author of *Look Homeward, Angel* and *Of Time and the River*, is going to end his series of four novels on American life in Oregon. The above-named stories have had wonderful sales and Oregon gets mention in *Of Time and the River*. The rough drafts of the other two, *The October Fair* and *The Hills Beyond Pentland*, have been completed and the North Carolina writer is now hewing them down. He usually writes a million words or more for a novel, then cuts down one-half.

"You see, part of our family left the hills of North Carolina and moved away west, going into Oregon," Mr. Wolfe explained, as he laid aside the proofs he had been reading. "They settled around Eugene—there's a lot of farming land around Eugene, isn't there?"

The 35-year-old bachelor novelist was assured there is, and very good farming land, too.

"Well, a big passel of my kin went out there," he continued, "and some of the best ones died there. I went west a few weeks ago and I wanted to get up to Oregon, but just couldn't get time."

"Why t' hell don't you come out here and live?" my people write me.

"I want to, but I've got to stay here and make a living. You know, every American is a westerner at heart. From the minute I got off the train in Colorado I felt right at home. I simply was sure I knew the place although it was the first time I was any farther west than Knoxville, Tenn."

Mr. Wolfe, whose recent novel, *Of Time and the River*, is more than 500,000 words long, is six feet six inches tall and of large frame. He doesn't like to sit down. He does all his writing standing up, corrects proofs that way and refuses to be seated when interviewed.

"My recent trip across the country was just to get a good look at the United States," this southern author explained. "I was born in Asheville, N.C., and didn't get to go any place until I was grown up. When I came to New York and began talking about wanting to see the rest of the country my friends here said all the rest of the United States looks alike, only New York is different.

"Say, such language as that is all in a white mule's ear. When it is ironed out you can see that this kind of talk is foolishness. San Francisco is no more like Cincinnati or Santa Fe is like Buffalo than Denmark is like the Holy Land. Maybe not as much. San Francisco is the most interesting and most exciting city I was ever in. It is a much more exciting town than Copenhagen, where I spent several weeks this spring and early summer. Now, Copenhagen has some real life, both day life and night life, let me tell you. But San Francisco is a city apart.

"Europe is grand and beautiful, but America is grander and more beautiful. And out of America is going to come some real art, great art, in literature and in music and in sculpture. There is a freshness here they don't have over there. In England and Denmark the grass you see looks like it was 400 years old."

Mr. Wolfe says the most difficult thing he has to do is to get back to work after a vacation trip. "I like to work after I get started," he declared as he began gathering up his proofs, and showed signs of wanting to get back to reading them. "They say I'm lazy, but I think a great deal of work in the world is done by lazy people, for when a lazy man gets the urge to work he goes after it harder than anyone else."

Author of several books as well as one of the most prolific writers among newspaper workers of the Pacific Northwest, David W. Hazen made himself a specialist in interviews. In an editorial tribute to him shortly after his death in 1944, the Oregonian *(February 28, 1944) referred to him as the American dean of interviewers: "Portland is not a crossroads for the great of the world, but Mr. Hazen made up for that by not missing any who did come. And he supplemented his amazing local collection by periodic trips around the country and even to Europe—each trip carefully planned as to the persons he was to see, so that no hour would lack its interview. It is doubtful whether any other journalist in the country had talked to so many of the great and the near great—the 'sinners and the saints,' as he called them." Hazen's interview with Thomas Wolfe in New York was followed by another three years later in Portland, Oregon.*

New York *Herald Tribune,* November 3, 1935

By the end of 1935, the name of Thomas Wolfe was well known in America. Of Time and the River had achieved great success, Wolfe was recognized everywhere he went, and at last he had money in his pockets.

Obviously Homer Bigart was aware of the Sanderson Vanderbilt interview in the New York Herald Tribune nine months earlier, and as a representative of the same newspaper, he had no intention of arousing Wolfe's ire a second time. On this occasion the novelist and the reporter had a friendly meeting, though the interview contains touches of sarcasm.

"Thomas Wolfe at 35 Is Tired of Being a Legend—'Wild Exuberance' of Figure in His Novels Changing to Concern over Work—Economizing on Words—New Book Only 304 Pages; Plans Million of Them" appeared with the same Zerbe photograph that accompanied the February 18, 1935, article in the New York Herald Tribune.

Thomas Wolfe is fed up with being a legend. At thirty-five he finds it increasingly difficult to live with the "wild exuberance" of Eugene Gant, chief figure of his novels *Look Homeward, Angel* and *Of Time and the River.* Yesterday he confessed that the goat cry wells less frequently in his throat.

As the Gant dies within, the Wolfe is becoming concerned about what the critics think of his books and what his public thinks of him. Frequently he hesitates in the middle of a sentence to inquire anxiously: "Will that look too boastful in print?" Even more significant is the change in his personal habits: he has taken to pressing his clothes and paying his phone bill.

Yesterday's interview was held in the offices of Charles Scribner's Sons, publishers of Wolfe's new book *From Death to Morning,* a collection of short stories that will appear November 14. Mr. Wolfe sat in a small, quiet, conventional library and in such surroundings he was ill at ease and for a while inarticulate. His six feet five inches frame was incased in a neat suit of blue serge; a remarkably thick knitted tie was tightly in place, and only his black hair was free from restraint. It swished freely above his ears, advertising to the world that its owner cared not a rap for surface impressions.

Mr. Wolfe was just back from a six-month vacation and according to his editors was "a lot less jumpy" than when he left Brooklyn after polishing off his 450,000-word *Of Time and the River*. First he toured Europe, then he came back and invaded the West. He failed to go down to Asheville, N.C., the "Altamont" of his books, and he said he hadn't seen the home town in five years.

"The folks in Asheville were pretty hot about *Look Homeward, Angel*," Mr. Wolfe admitted ruefully. "They all thought I'd written the town up, but someone told me recently that they had taken a kinder attitude."

What caused the loudest uproar, Mr. Wolfe said, was the scene in which he described the sale of a marble angel for the grave of a local lady of uneasy virtue. This was conceived as pure fiction, he explained, yet it set everyone in Asheville to guessing the identity of the woman. At length the city editor of the local paper sent a photographer to the graveyard. "He took a picture of the first damned angel he came to," said the author, "and it was over the grave of a perfectly good Methodist lady."

He confessed little desire to return to Asheville permanently. The place, he said, was full of tourists. He has "a hankering," however, to settle in Yancey County, which is about forty miles from Asheville and the original proving ground of his mother's family. "They are just mountain people in Yancey County," explained Mr. Wolfe, "but they are very good people too."

Mr. Wolfe's mother, who is seventy-six, came up to see him last week. She still lives in Asheville, although her real estate holdings, according to Mr. Wolfe, have been sadly hit by the Depression. Regarding his own finances, the author said the income from his novels, both best sellers, had enabled him to realize two ambitions: an apartment overlooking the East River and an occasional meal at Luchow's.

"People see your books in the best-seller lists and think you're getting hundreds of thousands of dollars," he added. "With reasonable luck I'll be able to get along a couple of years without worrying about rent, light and food."

Three weeks ago Mr. Wolfe passed his thirty-fifth birthday and the anniversary caused him to consider the rapid flight of time. With half a lifetime gone, his physical contribution to literature is a mere million words. "I've wasted too much time," he worried yesterday. "I've got to get back to work. I'm a sort of lazy person but, like most lazy people, I've got a prick of conscience and when it hurts too much I get going."

When Mr. Wolfe is writing, he usually "gets going" about noon. He has never learned to typewrite and nearly paralyzed his right arm while setting down the colossal *Of Time and the River* in longhand. He wrote the novel in a Brooklyn Heights apartment and his daily routine follows: "About noon the girl came in and we'd make coffee. I'd drink two pots. Some people knock it but I think it's grand stuff. Then I'd start to write. It would come hard at first and then around 4 o'clock it would come fast. Sometimes my mind worked like a triphammer and I'd get so tired I'd walk all over Brooklyn. I love to go around nights. Someday I'm going to write about nights."

Mr. Wolfe took occasion yesterday to set to rest two misconceptions which he feared had arisen from his last novel: hatred of Brooklyn, where he lived last year, and bad feeling toward New York University, where he taught English in 1927. "I think Brooklyn's swell," he enthused. "There's a whole universe of stuff to write about over there."

Now that he can look back over the years with detachment, Mr. Wolfe says N.Y.U. wasn't so bad after all. "I was treated by my employers with great kindness," he recalled. "I can look back over the years and say that I was treated all right. If I wasn't happy at teaching it was because I wanted to do something else."

Nothing so typifies the new restraint in Mr. Wolfe as the size of his forthcoming book, which is a mere 304 pages. It contains fourteen stories, some of which have been published in magazines. Only one of the pieces, "The Web of Earth," is related to the Gant-Pentland saga. "My tendency is to put in rather than take out," Mr. Wolfe confessed. "But the editors told me we ought to give the readers a break and give them a book like this."

Meanwhile Mr. Wolfe has completed the draft of his third novel of the Gants and the Pentlands. It is to be called *October Fair*, and the author wants to put six months' work on it before submitting it to Scribner's. He has also written about 500,000 words on the fourth novel, *The Hills Beyond Pentland*, which he feels will be the best of the series.

"I've got a hunch about that book," he said. "You know, sometimes you feel it gathering inside you. I want to work like hell on it for two years."

Mr. Wolfe said he wanted to thank the critics for telling him that his last book was too long.

"There are a million things I want to say," he said, "but I think I can say them with an economy of words."

Homer Bigart won a Pulitzer Prize in 1951 for "distinguished reporting on international affairs." He was a foreign correspondent for both the New York Herald Tribune *and the New York* Times.

New York *Post*, March 14, 1936

In early 1936, Wolfe met with the journalist May Cameron for an interview. The story goes that, perhaps remembering his outrage at Sanderson Vanderbilt (see New York Herald Tribune, February 18, 1935), Wolfe decided to avoid a personal confrontation and told the newspaperwoman that he would write out something and send it to her. The result was an article entitled "Thomas Wolfe Talks about His Contemporaries and Predicts a Bright Future for Our Writers—Author of Of Time and the River Feels Sure American Literature Is on the Verge of Its Most Striking Creative Period." It is possible but cannot be proved that, except for the first two paragraphs, the article consists of Wolfe's own carefully considered words. The inclusion of this quasi interview in Press Time: A Book of Post Classics (New York, 1936) omitted six paragraphs (now restored) from the newspaper version. Alexander D. Wainwright of Princeton, New Jersey, reports that in his collection there is a "typescript of the interview, which has extensive changes and additions in Wolfe's hand (in pencil)."

Today's column is devoted, with my warm thanks, to the author of *Look Homeward, Angel* and *Of Time and the River*. I asked Mr. Wolfe about his own work, about contemporary literature and writers and where American literature is heading.

The interview grew as abundant, as rich, it seemed to me, as pages of his own novels. Rather than confine Mr. Wolfe to the conventional question-and-answer pattern of an interview, I offer Thomas Wolfe speaking:

"I don't have any feeling about the success of another man other than the best kind of feeling in the world. It's really people who are unproductive, or in a nonproductive stage of life who have envious or morbidly acute feelings about other writers. Or what is worst of all, those wretched and unhappy creatures who are just half-productive—the half-artist longing for the whole—without the energy and power to achieve it. It's so ridiculous that it shouldn't even be mentioned in a newspaper to consider someone your rival. I'm not talking through my hat. I mean it, mean it seriously.

"Another thing, when you're producing you don't think about other people. You think about work, day in and day out, work. People have said about me that I have no critical faculty about my own work or any one else's, but I have a deep feeling about books.

"I have met both Hemingway and Faulkner and my own deep feeling is that neither has begun to reach full maturity and that both will do much better books than they have done yet. I always remember Hemingway's *In Our Time*, which was published very early in his career and doesn't seem to be well known. I felt in reading that book that here was a man who had roots in American life and obviously the man who had written that book had material for a grand book about American life. I've got a notion that some day he's going to write it.

"It's the same about Faulkner, whose talent is as different from Hemingway's as any talent could be; I don't think he has begun yet to use the whole range and sweep of his material, for here is a man whose talent could play over all of life. I've read *The Sound and the Fury* and *As I Lay Dying* and, of course, *Sanctuary*. I've no notion of how he will develop, but here is a man with too extensive knowledge to deal merely with the horrible and the demented and the macabre types of life. He has extensive knowledge of all types of humanity; I've felt that in every book of his I've ever read.

"In such a book as *As I Lay Dying* the reader feels not only the horror of a special situation but he feels also the grasp and knowledge that this man has of the humanity those people represent, which in this case was a family of farmers in Mississippi. I felt that, too, in *The Sound and the Fury*. *The Sound and the Fury* was in many ways a very wonderful book, and I doubt that a man of that imaginative and inventive power can be held down—as people have indicated—or restricted to one type of story. The thing in itself has the power to proliferate and extend itself indefinitely.

"I don't think that Hemingway's experiences and material ran out with the war. I've got a notion Hemingway's greatest work lies in this country, in his experiences, his memories and his imagination. I do feel this deeply from my own experience. I don't know whether today we've got any great writers in America—perhaps we haven't— but I do have almost an overwhelming feeling inside of me that we're going to produce wonderful books in the next twenty years. Just call it a hunch, because I couldn't prove it to clever critics, but it's a hell of a strong hunch. I don't think the lid has ever been taken off the pot here in America, and I think the day is coming when the lid will be pulled off.

"My own feeling is that America hasn't been written about yet. I've been reading *Life on the Mississippi,* and the first two hundred pages are as grand as anything ever can be, where Mark Twain tells of his childhood and his apprenticeship on a steamboat and the way he talks about the river; that river becomes a great poem and every time it touches his life and the lives of the people he tells about it becomes something magnificent.

"I'd never read Walt Whitman until after *Look Homeward, Angel* was published and when critics said I had been influenced by him I thought I'd better read him and find out how he had influenced me. We can be proud of Whitman—anybody can pick holes in him—but he's told about this country better than anybody I ever read, the way things are, behind the lines rather than in words, the shape and design of things in America.

"I do feel that today we have a kind of freedom from the superstitions and idolatries and false reverence of the past and I've found out we have to create a language, just as every literature with a new life and every new time and every new state of things—people will find their own language.

"It's going to come and I have no proof of it except the feeling in my blood and in my bones and in my brain. You had the beginning in Twain and Whitman, indications of what it may be, although it doesn't have to imitate. I just don't feel this life and this country have ever been expressed in that way or written about.

"My interest has been in subject matter, one reason that so many critics went for me about the number of words, too many adjectives and my lack of form. I haven't resented this: there's a lot of truth in it. Living abroad I saw concrete ways of civilization so different that I suppose my mind and memory and everything in me boiled over—I wanted to tell the way the pavement looks, the size and shape of the Sixth Avenue L and the way a forest looks in winter as you go through Maryland or Virginia. Then I tried to find a way of telling about those things.

"I don't know many writers. I've got a notion that when a man is creating something, that part of the literary world concerned with what critics say, what writers say about each other, is more remote from him than everybody else, even from people who read reviews. I've got a notion a lot of young fellows are doing what I did, each discovering in his own way his own world, his America, a big or little universe. The man who's creating is less tangled up in what somebody thinks of him in comparison to others than anybody else.

"I have a mania for figures, though I can't keep track of how much money I spend. I make long lists. Lists of the towns in America where I've been. Lists of towns and their populations and lists of places I want to see written about. When somebody does a book on New England I wonder what's wrong with the Rocky Mountains or Delaware. I'm delighted when I read a new book—a very good book—about some part of America that has not been dealt with before; it gives me a kind of good feeling when I think of something else in America being written about.

"Ten or twelve years ago everybody had the idea that if you wanted to write you had to go to Paris, and I went. Probably what saved me was that I didn't know any literary groups, and I worked. People don't go away to write any more, but I do know that by going away I came to have a feeling about America that I had never had before.

"Sometimes in the last few years people have asked me what I thought about 'proletarian literature' and some have accused me, in criticisms or letters, of lacking what they call 'social consciousness.' I can't say as to this, because I think what I write will have to answer for me, and I think that, like every other writer who ever lived, I'll have to stand or fall by what I write. But I will say this:

"My people were all working people, had to work for their livings, and my natural instinctive feeling is on the side of the working class. But the life of an artist depends upon his knowledge of people. They may call you an autobiographical writer, may point out your weaknesses, but you can't go anywhere with your work until you know your people to the bottom, know them as well as if you were the source and the root, as if their lives came out of yourself. How can you deal with social conditions, or economic situations, or with people placed in this position because of a structure of society unless you know your people to the core with more exactness than a scientist's knowledge?

"I fail to see why social consciousness should be construed as meaning a particular set of dogmas.

"I went abroad a year ago after a period of four or five years' work, felt done for, worn out, no hope for the book, no idea of its reception except a crashing failure. A lot of that was physical reaction. It was wonderful to come back and find I had some little recognition. It took four or five days for that to soak into me and all the time it was like being full of champagne and feeling good all the time. It was the greatest happiness, but to tell the truth I'm tired of it now.

"A writer when he's young thinks that fame is what he's after. He sets too high a value on success—the praise, the profits and the women—but as he gets older, he finds the thing he longs for most desperately is to grow, to perfect his work, to increase the power and scope of his experience. I am thirty-five years old, and I would be untruthful if I said I did not still like the kind of success I have mentioned, but I don't think it means as much to me as it once did.

"At twenty or twenty-one I thought I was as sharp as hell, could absorb whole philosophies and economic doctrines one right after the other. But now things go banging off about my head, and as far as these ideas have any value they have got to come through the slow process of growth. As far as creative writing goes, you've got to use what is your own. The very young writer deals with naked facts of his own experience, puts in Bill Jones or Tom Grant—often a thinly disguised version of what he may think of himself—then groups his story around this figure. And right here, I could say this about 'autobiographical writing' and 'autobiographical writers'—I've often been accused of being one: I think that often the reason a man is an 'autobiographical writer' (and every man *is* one in one way or another) is not because that man wants to justify himself, or make a hero of himself, but just because he is a writer with the will and urge to write, a man who *has* to write, and yet has never written, and so knows nothing about writing, and so puts in a figure called Bill Jones or Tom Grant, just because that is the easiest way he can begin, a kind of handle he can hold to.

"As you go on, what you write becomes less concerned with Bill as a person to justify yourself and you're able to enlarge upon experience so that Bill's or Tom's experience becomes interesting and significant to you only in terms of its relation to general humanity, in terms of consonance to general humanity, and if that's not social consciousness, I don't know what the hell it is.

"Whatever you write has got to come out of your life. You can't write of what you don't know about and that doesn't belong to you: you've got to write about what you do know and that does belong to you. You're not going to come back from four or five months in Europe a changed person. I can't swallow things whole; I've got to sweat and labor. An artist has got to grow or he's done for, and growth is not a rapid thing; neither do I believe in sudden conversion, or revelation from the Mount of Saint Swithin. This is truer for the artist, I think, than for any one else. There are people who absorb things overnight, but in the end it might work out that some of the others who have to sweat it out our own way may cut a deeper furrow.

"The writer of twenty or twenty-two who's creating is a hell of an egotist, with a chip on one shoulder. If anyone says he can't write, he becomes more arrogant, carrying on in a high-handed way, looking at all life as a reflection of his own personality. As you grow older you begin to lose that. I've done a good deal of sweating about things around me and I've a deeper and wider feeling about them and it didn't come because I read it in a book. Those things come from the processes of living, sweating and experiencing.

"I think that a book has to stand upon the talent of its author. You may have a great proletarian novelist, or a great religious novelist, or a great historical novelist, but first of all you've got to have a great novelist, and anything, from a proletarian to a religious novel, that will extend the variety and range of literature is a thing that should be developed."

Berliner Tageblatt, August 5, 1936

In early August the Olympic games were in full swing. Every afternoon Hitler sat in his box at the stadium. A day or so before Wolfe was interviewed, the American trio of Jesse Owens, Ralph Metcalfe, and Frank Wykoff had come in first, second, and fourth in the finals of the hundred-meter race.

In spite of the excitement of the Olympics, Berlin in 1936 was not for Wolfe the exhilarating experience of the year before. His friends were guarded and cautious in what they said, and an indefinable fear permeated the city. Even so, for a while, Wolfe's restless effervescence persisted, somewhat blotting out the ominous presence of the ubiquitous military.

Heinz Ledig-Rowohlt, son of Wolfe's German publisher, arranged for him to be interviewed in his room at the Hotel am Zoo on the Kurfürstendamm. The article was titled "Wir sprachen Thomas Wolfe." The journalist H. H. (otherwise unidentified) brought along a tall, beautiful Prussian blonde, who caught Wolfe's eye at once. Her name was Thea Voelcker, and she was to make a drawing of Wolfe to accompany the printed interview. Wolfe was immediately enchanted by this handsome Valkyrie and so completely distracted by her that the questions he was asked received brief and often disconnected answers. Several times his friend Ledig-Rowohlt had to tell the interviewer anecdotes about Wolfe (the Oktoberfest brawl, the haberdasher story) to make up for Wolfe's absentminded responses.

See Richard S. Kennedy and Paschal Reeves (eds.), The Notebooks of Thomas Wolfe *(Chapel Hill, 1970), 818; H. M. Ledig-Rowohlt, "Thomas Wolfe in Berlin,"* American Scholar, *XXII (Spring, 1953), 185–201.*

If his curly hair is included, he is all of two meters [six feet, six inches] tall. From that height he commands a magnificent view of the world around him. Thomas Wolfe also has magnificent prospects: he is thirty-five years old, has a solid reputation, a healthy appetite and, thank God, not too much money as yet. He is tense and full of energy.

Thea Voelcker's drawing of Thomas Wolfe

What he sees, hears, feels, and writes, he sees, hears, feels, and writes from his sense of exuberance. One might say it is his craft.

The basic characteristics of this gigantic youth are his boyishness, his naïveté. He is free of prejudice, is not selfish or conceited, and does not engage in idle chatter or pompous statements like so many famous youths. When he thinks he is laughing too loud, he bashfully bends his head and the muffled undertones sound like sobbing. It is an affecting moment for us.

We ask what he thinks of German literature. "Goethe personifies for me the idea of world literature." His statement is one of strong conviction.

"As a child? Ah, as a child I delivered newspapers. Later I went to Harvard University and became a teacher. Then I wrote a play, but it was miserable. Later on, with prose, I fared better."

"Berlin?" The question is obligatory.

"Marvelous. If there were no Germany, it would be necessary to invent one. It is a magical country. I know Hildersheim, Nuremberg, Munich, the architecture of Germany, the soul of the place, the glory of her history and art."

Suddenly we hear the shouts of a news vendor in the streets, announcing a fresh supply of gold medals at the Olympic stadium. Wolfe searches his pocket for a coin to buy a newspaper.

America? Thomas Wolfe (whose life-size picture, if you don't know him personally, could easily be taken for a larger-than-life monument to himself—or so it seems to us) is, we are aware, thoroughly patriotic. Owens, Metcalfe, Wykoff! I comment that at one whack it's three times America. I am puzzled when Wolfe turns to me with a blank expression and says, "Two hundred years ago my forefathers emigrated from southern Germany to America." Apparently he has forgotten the Olympics entirely.

We learn that eight years before his current visit he took a beautiful tour through the Black Forest. He went on to Munich and was there at the time of the Oktoberfest. In a beer hall at the festival grounds, a neighbor to his right on the bench tapped him gently on the chest as if to say, "You are really a fine fellow." Wolfe tapped his neighbor kindly in return, the neighbor again, Wolfe once more—and it all finally ended in an Oktoberfest brawl! Of course the brawl grew out of a mutual misunderstanding, but the smashed beer mug on the author's head caused him to spend a few days in the hospital under the care of the famous Doktor Geheimrat Lexer.

It seems hardly conceivable that this peaceable man, almost clumsy, only marginally inclined toward alcohol, a man who has conversations with his friends the sparrows and the finches—that such a man could find himself engaged in an Oktoberfest brawl. The psychological contrast between the Munich fracas and the gentle character of the man makes the beer-hall fight, in a certain sense, a tragic, certainly a moving event, however comical it may appear to be *post festum*.

Of a similar "tragic" incident, we don't know how to tell without being too explicit. Recently, when planning to attend an official Berlin reception for Charles Lindbergh, Wolfe discovered he needed a new shirt. But buying one was another matter entirely. The haberdasher could hardly have foreseen the extraordinary measurements of the American author. Regrettably the sleeves reached only to the elbows; nor could, what follows logically, the other dimensions of the pattern satisfy half the requirements. That which under normal circumstances should have been a comic situation, an oversight, a modest joke perhaps, turned out to be an exasperating predicament for Wolfe. The dilemma was caused, we suspect, because the shy, embarrassed fellow did not dare say to the saleslady: "But, my dear lady, that funny thing there is, for my proportions, only a bib." What is a simple transaction for the average person, for Wolfe is a basic problem.

In none of his emotions and enthusiasms does he seem to be false or insincere. Casually he says, "The Kurfürstendamm is so beautifully quiet"—while, even as he speaks the words, people from all nations are swarming on the streets below. "Here I can relax. We Americans, for our inner balance, need this peaceful, restful atmosphere."

"What do you think of sports?"

"Oh, I like them. I do a great deal of walking." He tells us that all alone, without a companion, he strolls throughout Berlin. This way, he says, he can better grasp and understand people and things.

Yes, at one time he was in Hollywood. "Money is quite nice, but it's not everything."

Wolfe gets out of his chair and, from his towering two meters, he watches the throng of people from the window. He enjoys the "peaceful" scene.

"I am working on six books, you know, so I need this vacation."

One should not take too seriously Wolfe's statement about the emigration of his ancestors to America two hundred years ago. Yet, when he stands there before us, one feels that Albrecht Dürer might have drawn just such a head as his. One thinks, too, that at that moment the American writer looks rather like a peasant farmer from southern Germany, perhaps like Richard Billinger, the Bavarian writer of country life, only more manly, forceful, and rustic.

When Wolfe saw the interview, he complained bitterly about the drawing, which he said gave him a Schweinsgesicht *(swine's face). But a week later, his anger abated, he again met Thea Voelcker. Immediately a frenzied but brief love affair began, and the two went off on a trip to the Austrian Tyrol. In chapters 38 through 40 of* You Can't Go Home Again *the character Franz Heilig is based on Heinz Ledig-Rowohlt and Else von Kohler on Thea Voelcker.*

On September 8, on his way by train to Paris, at the border crossing into Belgium at Aachen, Wolfe witnessed an episode which he later wrote up as "I Have a Thing to Tell You." In Germany he had known fame and love, but after Aachen he would never go back.

The translation of this interview from the German was made by Professor Klaus Lanzinger of the University of Notre Dame.

Times-Picayune New Orleans States, January 3, 1937

The New Orleans trip came at a difficult time in Wolfe's career. He had become convinced that he could no longer remain with Maxwell Perkins at Scribner's, and in New York City he was unable to escape his emotional depression. And so he turned south. See Elizabeth Nowell, Thomas Wolfe (Garden City, N.Y., 1960), 364–70.

In February, 1909, he and his mother had been in New Orleans at the time of Mardi Gras, visiting his first cousin William Oliver Wolfe II, called Ollie, his wife Effie, and daughter Mary Louise. Also in the house were Ollie's parents Wesley and Aurelia Wolfe and two bachelor brothers. This time Wolfe's arrival in the city on New Year's Eve coincided with that of the crowd attending the Sugar Bowl football game.

Thomas Sancton's "Thomas Wolfe Revisits City Whose Spirit He Portrayed in First Successful Novel—Delineator of Dixie Life Still Seeking 'Open Sesame' That Will Unlock World, He Shyly Reveals" was a front-page feature story. Heading it was a full-face "Photo by The Times-Picayune" with a cutline stating that Wolfe, "acclaimed as one of America's greatest writers, is in New Orleans for a short while to rest."

Twenty-seven years ago, when he was nine years old, Thomas Wolfe of Asheville, N.C., came with his mother to New Orleans and lived for a short while in the home of a cousin, a plasterer, on Merigny Street. He saw the French market, heard and remembered the bayou patois of his cousin's cook, thought one night a trembler had struck the city when his aunt's snoring rattled the window frames. Later he put all this in a book.

That book was *Look Homeward, Angel*, a story of the inner life of a Southern boy. It became famous, and Wolfe a celebrated author. Saturday he was in New Orleans for the first time since the childhood visit, exhausted from a creative spurt which ended Christmas morning, and seeking rest.

With "another 48 hours' sleep" as his immediate goal, he moved Saturday to The Roosevelt from a boarding house where he stayed in comparative seclusion since his arrival here Thursday.

He plans to leave soon for his first visit to Asheville in seven years. His first novel, based on personal experiences, was filled with hometown background. The setting was a fictitious city called Altamont, but Asheville residents, many of them, felt that the work had bared its citizenry to unsympathetic outside curiosity.

On the basis of *Look Homeward, Angel*, Sinclair Lewis, on receipt of the Nobel prize for literature, said Wolfe showed promise of becoming the outstanding American man of letters of all time. But hometowners thought differently. Wolfe was in the North at the time of publication and word drifted up that the town was mad at him.

"One dear old lady wrote that I'd better keep my 'overgrown carkus' where it would be safe," he said. And so he went into a sort of exile.

"But that has all changed now," he said Saturday. "Asheville has been through a boom and a depression. The people have forgotten a lot and come to understand much more. I've been invited to give a lecture there and so I'm going home for a while, and glad to go."

Wolfe's first novel was followed by a series of "short stories," which were more or less plotless descriptions of American and European experiences. Several years ago *Of Time and the River*, a continuation of his earlier novel, was published, and generally acclaimed by critics. Among other things, he was described as "the Walt Whitman of the novel."

Wolfe is a towering man, well over six feet and heavy. He has an air of startling modesty, which in conversation crops out in phrases such as "if I become an established writer," and "when I learn to write."

He scrawls his work in pencil on piles of wrapping paper, sometimes at the rate of 6000 words a day. His first novel was penciled in ledger books.

The work which he finished Christmas was, for him, a departure into complete fiction. He wrote it in the kitchen of a little Brooklyn flat, where, he says, he does his best work. The book is tentatively called *The Hound of Darkness*.

"It is," he says, "a story of the year 1916 in a Southern town, of the lives of a group of young men unaware that they are being ambushed by the World War. It ends with what I guess will be called a daring scene, the picture of America in the moonlight waiting for the war—of leaves rustling over the continent."

Through his work runs a recurring chant in praise of the "American earth": of trains, mountains, dialects and place names.

"We haven't done it yet," he said Saturday, "but we're going to produce a great literature. There is a brutal beauty in America. Not so much the beauty of graceful plantation manors and the like but the beauty of desolate country, of unpainted barns and red clay earth."

During the last eight years he has written about 5,000,000 words, of which about one-fifth has been published.

"Maybe some of that one-fifth shouldn't have been published," he said. "I can't build up slowly and carefully; I've got to pour it out. It's that or nothing.

"A man can't help writing about things he's done and seen and people he's known. No matter how much you want to create you have to be autobiographical. You can't pull it out of the air. It's got to come from the inside, and what you got there is autobiography. And if you know these things to be true, if you write the truth about a man, you can't hurt him."

The artist, Mr. Wolfe believes, must steer clear of dogma and "movements" to survive. He has no faith in the value of "snug little schools of writing and literary publication dedicated to the advancement of a restricted point of view."

Wolfe was graduated at the University of North Carolina at Chapel Hill, then attended Harvard University for three years. He went to Europe to write his first novel and has spent many years traveling there since its publication. For a time he taught literature at a New York university.

In his writing, he has repeated a poignant desire for a "key" into the realm of artistic and intellectual satisfaction, a desire to find "a stone, a leaf, a door" that will prove the "open Sesame" into this world.

"If one ever finds it," he said, "I suppose it will be in his work, in a sense of growth and completion. I am still looking."

When word got around that Wolfe was in New Orleans, he was courted right and left. The local literary set, book collector William B. Wisdom, old friends from Asheville, and especially newspaper reporters all kept him busy. Along the streets in the French Quarter he was soon a familiar figure. One of the bartenders remembered him as the "big guy in the tux who couldn't dance to the piano because he couldn't get his big feet off the floor."

Among his drinking cronies was "Fatty" McDermott, who got the idea that Wolfe was a sportswriter. No, said Wolfe, the only newspaper work he ever did was to deliver the Asheville Citizen *on cold, dark mornings. "Don't kid me," said McDermott, "you're a baseball writer, and your father owns the* Citizen." *With that Wolfe grabbed a newspaper, folded it the way newsboys do, and threw it with deadly accuracy against the barroom wall. "See that. I'm the best damned newspaper boy the Asheville* Citizen *ever had, I'll tell you that much." On another occasion when he was drinking with a reporter, McDermott picked up the reporter's copy of* Look Homeward, Angel *and read a passage. "That's a lot of tripe, a lot of bosh," he announced. Wolfe took the book from him, opened it to the proem, and intoned those famous words: " 'O lost, and by the wind grieved, ghost, come back again.' Tripe," said Wolfe, "and bosh. I never read such bosh in my life. Rack 'em up," he told the bartender.*

One morning at eight o'clock after a long barhopping night in the Quarter, he was standing on the grassy levee alongside the Mississippi at Audubon Park. With him was a group of new friends. Wolfe picked up a tuft of grass, held it high, and watched as the wind blew it away from his open palm. "This, fellows, this is America," he boomed, "and that river is some river." "Shucks," a reporter countered, "you ought to see it in high water." See William H. Fitzpatrick, "Thomas Wolfe, Author, Dies; Visit Here in 1937 Recalled," New Orleans Times-Picayune, *September 16, 1938, and Thomas Sancton, "Time and the River,"* New Orleans Item, *October 26, 1950.*

Thomas Sancton, a Neiman Fellow at Harvard in 1941–1942, was a teacher, political reporter, novelist, and later vice-president of a public relations firm.

Atlanta *Constitution,* January 17, 1937

Wolfe was so exhausted after more than a week of New Orleans hospitality that he retreated to Biloxi, Mississippi, for several days of sleep. In Atlanta on his way to New Orleans, he had stopped just long enough to get in touch with two college friends from Chapel Hill days, Ernest Henry Abernethy and Garland B. Porter, and to promise them a visit on his return. After Biloxi, Wolfe headed northeast to keep his promise. "'Of Time and the River's' Author Hopes for Time to Read 'Gone'" was written by Lee Fuhrman.

Speaking volubly, dynamically, Thomas Wolfe, famous southern author of *Look Homeward, Angel* and *Of Time and the River,* last night revealed he had not yet read Margaret Mitchell's best-selling novel *Gone with the Wind.*

"I just haven't got around to it," said Wolfe, when asked if he had read the Atlanta writer's work, sales of which are straggling around the million mark. "I am anxious to read it, yes," he continued. "I understand it is a fine piece of work. I had hoped to meet Miss Mitchell, too, and friends tried to arrange it during my brief stay in this city. But I anticipate meeting her, and probably will, in New York."

Wolfe, who paused briefly in Atlanta to visit friends, principally E. H. Abernethy, Atlanta magazine publisher, and Garland Porter, advertising man, said he had completed the rough draft of his new book *The Hound of Darkness.* "I've been working on it for the past three months," he said, "and have written more than 300,000 words in that time. So you see, I've been busy. But the work is far from completed. The rough draft, that's about all."

Wolfe came here from New Orleans, and had high praise for southern hospitality.

"Everyone has been most kind and hospitable, and I appreciate deeply all that has been done for me. I'm tired, but it's mighty good to be home. In the south, I mean. This is my first trip south in seven years. It is just a trip for relaxation and to visit old friends." Wolfe will leave today for visits to friends in Chapel Hill, N.C., where he attended the University of North Carolina, Raleigh and Asheville, where he was born in 1900.

Besides his novels, which he writes in pencil, Wolfe, tall, heavy-set, electric, has written several plays, mainly for production by the Carolina Playmakers. He received a master of arts degree from Harvard, and in 1930 was awarded the Guggenheim Fellowship for creative writing.

Literary critics place his work on the same shelves with writings of Sinclair Lewis and Theodore Dreiser. He is one of a group of southern writers which has placed this section in the literary forefront within the past decade.

In the Atlanta Sunday American *on January 17, 1937, Paul Stevenson reported Wolfe as saying, "After weathering the hospitality of New Orleans, where I have spent several days, it's quite a task to face Atlanta's famous hospitality, but I'll try to bear up under the strain." Atlanta's hospitality was highly satisfactory, if considerably different. At Garland B. Porter's home, "Dinner the first evening was typical North Carolina fare: fried chicken, snap beans cooked with a slab of streak-of-fat-streak-of-lean, candied yams, fruit salad, and plenty of biscuits and gravy." Wolfe consumed several bountiful servings. He told Porter and his family, "You've got to excuse me, but this is the first real meal I've had in years—this is the kind of food I was raised on." See Andrew Turnbull,* Thomas Wolfe *(New York, 1967), 253.*

Lee Fuhrman, city editor of the Constitution, *wrote a comedy about newspaper life,* The Local Angle, *which was produced in 1952.*

Raleigh *News and Observer*, January 22, 1937

From Atlanta, Wolfe returned to North Carolina after an absence of seven years. First he visited in Southern Pines, then spent a night in Raleigh. In nearby Chapel Hill he remained for a long weekend and Monday morning spoke before a student group on the campus of the university. (See the article by George Stoney that is the last piece in this collection.) After a stopover in Warrenton with his college friend William Polk, he went back to New York. The Raleigh morning newspaper ran an interview by Clifton Daniel headlined "Tom Wolfe Is Ready To Trade Forgiveness—But Author of Long Books Hasn't Time for Long Books Like 'Gone With the Wind.'"

Tom Wolfe was in Raleigh last night, and he's going back to Asheville.

"I'm not afraid of being tar and feathered and run out of town, anymore," said the huge, shaggy-headed fellow who is North Carolina's best known—and undoubtedly, greatest—novelist.

He wagged his head and raked his fingers through his hair—nervously as he thought about it—how he wrote his first novel and a sensationally successful one, *Look Homeward, Angel,* about the people of Asheville and Chapel Hill and Raleigh.

And how he felt when he got that first letter, seven years ago, from an old lady in Asheville who had seen an advance copy of the book, an old lady who always had thought he was the finest boy of all.

And how they all said, hundreds of them in their letters, that the book was dirty and insulting and mean.

And how—"If Asheville took it hard," Wolfe said last night, "that was nothing compared to the way I took it. You know, you only have one home and one State, and when they take that away from you, well—if Asheville is willing to call it a draw, I certainly am."

Since *Look Homeward, Angel* appeared, Asheville has been

through a boom and a depression, worse calamities than having a
book written about you.

And Tom Wolfe's older, too, 36 now. "And I've learned a lot of
things," he said. Another book or two and many short stories, most
of them published in *Scribner's*, have been added to his list of pub-
lications, many thousands of miles to his travels in the years away
from home.

He's been so busy, he hasn't read Margaret Mitchell's *Gone with
the Wind*. They asked him about that, as they ask everybody, in Atlanta, recently. But he told them, "Hell, I haven't got time to read a
book that long."

And the joke is that his latest novel, *Of Time and the River*, is
only a few pages shorter. "One good thing about writing books is
that you don't have to read them," he said.

For months he has been slaving at a new novel, to be published in
April. When he's finished with it, he's going back to Asheville, back
to the mountains in the Spring.

His visit to Raleigh and North Carolina at this gray season was an
afterthought. "I went to New Orleans to rest, of all places," he explained last night, as he sat at supper with J. Maryon Saunders,
alumni secretary of the University of North Carolina, who was
taking him to Chapel Hill for the first time since his graduation there
in 1920.

"It's a grand town," he continued, talking about New Orleans, "but
it makes New York look like a country village. We do go to bed up
there, occasionally."

Then, too, he made the front pages of the papers in New Orleans
and the folks down there just about killed him with kindness. They
flocked to see him.

So, he beat a retreat to Southern Pines and the easy hospitality of
the home of James Boyd, author of *Drums* and other novels. From
there, after three nights of sound sleep, he came to Raleigh and from
here he went to the Hill.

Wolfe arrived in Raleigh at 2 A.M. Thursday and hung out the "Do
Not Disturb" card in his hotel. He arose at 4 P.M. yesterday and

went down for breakfast at 4:30. At 6 he was having dinner. He was not recognized generally in the hotel—not even in Raleigh, where certain people identified in the college-days section of his *Look Homeward, Angel* still live.

"This is a swell place," he said last night, after looking at the place for the first time since 1920. "It hasn't changed a bit, thank God."

A waitress told him that was heresy, but he laughed and added, "They haven't even swept out the railroad station." (Tom Wolfe is always noticing things about railways. Some folks say his descriptions of trains and people on trains are the best things he does.)

He expects to find Chapel Hill the same, too. "They can't change the landscape," he said.

Nor can they change the majesty of the mountains that he has missed all these years in New York and Europe. "Some day," he said, dipping his spatulalike fingers into the glass of ice water for the last time, picking up the gutted package of cigarettes from the table, "I'm going back to Yancey County, where my mother's family came from, to live."

From 1934 to 1937, Clifton Daniel was a reporter for the News and Observer *in Raleigh. He then went to New York and worked for the Associated Press. From 1944 until his retirement, he was with the New York* Times. *His wife, Margaret Truman, has written several books, including the mystery novel* Murder in the White House *(1980).*

During the last year of Wolfe's life, Daniel again met his fellow North Carolinian, and he "and a few others would sometimes go out drinking until dawn with Wolfe at bars in mid-Manhattan, later taking long walks on Broadway listening to the towering novelist sound off on a thousand subjects, monologues that went on and on through the street noise and passing crowds, under the bright theater marquees and tall buildings, and as Daniel strained to listen he realized that Thomas Wolfe talked as he wrote, the words streaming endlessly within a low tone of tension. While never a close friend, Daniel thought he knew Wolfe fairly well at this time, but then one night at a restaurant, after joining

Wolfe at a table, Daniel could tell from the way the conversation went that Wolfe had no recollection of ever having seen him before. Wolfe was drinking heavily then, and later that year he died." See Gay Talese, The Kingdom and the Power *(New York, 1969), 63–64.*

Bristol *News*, April 30, 1937

In the spring of 1937 Wolfe decided the time had come to end his exile of more than seven years from his hometown. Instead of a frontal approach, he concluded it was better to arrive cautiously by the back way. Without notifying his family of his intention, he began "loafing down the beautiful Shenandoah Valley" of Virginia, stopping occasionally as inclination dictated, and came to Bristol, straddling the Tennessee-Virginia line. He paid a visit to the novelist Anne W. Armstrong, who lived nearby, and in the town he met with a reporter from the small daily newspaper. See Anne W. Armstrong, "As I Saw Thomas Wolfe," Arizona Quarterly, II (Spring, 1946), 5–15. The unsigned article was titled "Thos. Wolfe, Famous Author, Visitor Here."

Thomas Wolfe, considered as one of the greatest living authors, was so fascinated by Bristol while here today that he stated he might return later in the summer and make temporary dwelling either in the city or in a cabin somewhere in the nearby mountains.

The noted writer arrived here from New York by bus last night and registered at the General Shelby Hotel. He will depart this evening for Asheville, N.C., where he will visit with his 77-year-old mother.

Several Bristolians who were thrilled by the reading of *Look Homeward, Angel, Of Time and the River,* and other works of Mr. Wolfe, visited him in his hotel room and found the 36-year-old novelist, who weighs 240 pounds and is 6 feet, 6 inches in height, as interesting in conversation as in his writings.

He described his return to his "homeland" after several years in New York and travels abroad as an "exciting experience."

"One has to go away," he said, "before he learns how deeply he is attached to his own people and own country."

Reprinted by permission of Bristol Newspapers, Inc.

He said he would spend about two weeks in North Carolina and then return to New York, but was "coming back" again when the hot days set in on that city.

"One of the first things I'm going to do," he said, "is to buy myself a second-hand car.

"I'll have to learn to drive first though," he added, "as that is one thing I have never done."

Wolfe, of whom Heywood Broun, one of the nation's outstanding columnists, said was "the American novelist," is one of the most prolific writers in the world, sometimes writing as much as 5,000 words a day. He has written more than a half million words during the past six months, now being engaged on a book of complete fiction, which he believes will be his best, and which probably will be published in four volumes.

His first novel *Look Homeward, Angel* was written eight years ago while he was an instructor at New York University. He sat up nights to write the book, based on his experiences while a youth in Asheville and while at the University of North Carolina. *Of Time and the River* was a continuation, experiences during his Harvard days and while in Europe. Two others in the same series, *The October Fair* and *The Hills Beyond Pentland*, will not be published until after the completion of the book he is working upon at present.

Other works of Mr. Wolfe include a book of stories *From Death to Morning*, a short book *The Story of a Novel*, a large number of short stories, including a recent short novel *I Have a Thing to Tell You*, based on the author's observations in Germany and published recently in three installments in *New Republic*.

In commenting on the earlier books, Wolfe stated his belief that in reality all books were autobiographical.

"All we have," he said, "is the experience of our own life and the power to use it. This is especially true in the case of writers."

He warned young writers, however, to beware of too closely identifying actual people and events. He said that even when a writer used careful disguise or their scenes and events were entirely imagi-

nary, ofttimes people would claim that they had been "stepped upon."
He said that a number of persons expressed themselves as "out-
raged" over references to personalities in *Look Homeward, Angel*,
which in truth were fiction characters created in his own mind.

Asheville *Times*, May 4, 1937

From Bristol, Wolfe slipped down into North Carolina. At Burnsville, he visited his half-great-uncle John B. Westall, aged ninety-five, and from him heard a Civil War reminiscence later used as the basis for his story "Chickamauga." On Monday, Wolfe reached Asheville, thirty miles away, and telephoned his surprised mother from downtown. It was a tumultuous homecoming. The native son had been forgiven, and for a week he was the center of attention among the same home folks who once had censored him.

"Thomas Wolfe Welcomed by Friends Here—Man Who Wrote 'Look Homeward, Angel' Happy to Be Back Home" was unsigned. Accompanying the interview was a photograph of Wolfe and his mother on the porch of 48 Spruce Street.

Thomas Wolfe, whose last visit to Asheville seven-and-a-half years ago saw him a young university professor with a bulky manuscript his chief claim to literary fame, came back to his home town a famous author and was acclaimed by a multitude of friends and autograph seekers.

The manuscript *Look Homeward, Angel* was published shortly afterwards and Mr. Wolfe advanced to the front rank of modern American writers.

"It's grand to be back," Mr. Wolfe told newspapermen this morning. "I feel good every time I see something familiar," he said, recalling that the buildings on the north side of Pack Square are much the same as [in] the days he was a boy growing up here.

"I feel perfectly at home," he continued. "You can't change the mountains," he added as an afterthought.

All morning the telephone rang at the home of Mr. Wolfe's mother, Mrs. Julia E. Wolfe, of 48 Spruce Street, as friends and well-wishers called to welcome the author home. Many called in person, and at one time there were as many as six persons waiting to see Mr. Wolfe.

Mr. Wolfe came to Asheville yesterday afternoon from Burnsville, in Yancey county, where he spent a few days enroute here.

Early this morning, he arose and walked to the home of his sister here, Mrs. R. H. Wheaton, of 201 Charlotte Street, where he later received newspapermen over a cup of coffee at the breakfast table.

Mr. Wolfe said he was looking for a small place in the mountains to which he could return this summer, probably the end of June, and work. "I don't want anything touristy," he explained, "but just a small place. I am getting fed up with all the noise and roar of New York, although living in New York is a grand experience."

Mr. Wolfe, six feet and five-and-a-half inches tall and weighing 240 pounds, dominated the breakfast table. As he talked over his coffee and cigarette, three members of the American Business club came in to ask him to address the meeting of the club today.

One of the three—James S. Howell—was an old friend of Mr. Wolfe's. "I can't make a talk," Mr. Wolfe told Mr. Howell. "You know the Wolfes were always tongue-tied." Finally, Mr. Wolfe agreed to make a short talk.

Returning to his mother's home on Spruce Street, the author found other friends waiting in the sun parlor of the home, where his diplomas from the University of North Carolina and Harvard University hung on the wall. In a bookcase were copies of *Look Homeward, Angel*, *Of Time and the River*, and others of his writings.

Arriving by bus yesterday from Burnsville, Mr. Wolfe took a taxi from the bus terminal to his mother's home. "Aren't you one of the Wolfe boys?" the author said the taxi driver asked. Receiving an affirmative answer, the driver continued, "I thought you talked like one of the Wolfe boys." Then he asked, "What became of your brother who sold the *Saturday Evening Post*?"

Yesterday and early this morning, the author walked over many sections of the city, visiting old and familiar places. He stopped by the old Wolfe residence on Woodfin Street and followed the paper route he once carried out Charlotte Street for The Asheville Citizen.

Until he leaves for New York the latter part of this week, Mr. Wolfe said he plans to visit around the city and drive out into the country. "I hope I don't have to make any more speeches," he said, "but I do want to see everybody."

Asked for comment on the awarding of the Pulitzer prize last night to Margaret Mitchell for her *Gone With the Wind*, Mr. Wolfe said he was glad to hear of Miss Mitchell's good fortune. He said he bought a copy of the book in Roanoke, Va., on his trip to this section, and planned to read it.

Formerly, Mr. Wolfe said he read everything, but now reads very few current books. On this trip he brought along copies of the Bible, Shakespeare, the *World Almanac*, *David Copperfield*, *Don Quixote*, and an old school textbook on French literature.

He finds relaxation in reading the almanac. "After a hard day's grind on imaginative work, there is something relaxing about cold hard figures," he explained. "Too, I am interested in baseball and I like sometimes to find out what Babe Ruth hit in 1927. I have a curious interest in figures and a passion for travel, so I like to know how many people there are in a town, its industries and such as I travel."

Mr. Wolfe, in answer to a question, said he was not afraid of running out of material for his books. He has completed rough drafts of two novels to go in the *Of Time and the River* series. The series is to consist of six books and the two have had *October Fair* and *The Hills Beyond Pentland* tentatively selected as their titles. Another probably will be known as *Hounds of Darkness*.

Mr. Wolfe's first book *Look Homeward, Angel*, when it first appeared in 1929, aroused considerable feeling in Asheville because it contained characters which many persons said were residents of this city. The author made no apology for his book. He did say, however, that he was sorry if he had displeased anyone.

"If anything I have ever written has displeased anyone in Asheville I hope that I shall be able to write another book which will please them," he said.

On the same day as the Times *interview, the Asheville* Citizen *ran a first-page two-column story "Thos. Wolfe Comes Home for First Time Since Writing Novel." In it Wolfe was quoted as saying that his arrival in Asheville climaxed an "exciting trip. . . . I was coming home. I was renewing my connections with my own neck of the woods." The anonymous reporter noted that Wolfe was "well over six feet and is heavily built. At present, his hair is quite long but he says he is going to get a haircut today. As he answered questions for the* Citizen *interviewer, he paced the floor, not nervously, but restlessly. He appeared to be greatly affected by his return to Asheville and gave the impression that he was deeply sincere and earnest about what he was saying."*

Just before leaving for New York, he was asked by his friend the journalist George W. McCoy to write something of his feelings at being home again, of how he now looked upon Asheville's reaction to Look Homeward, Angel *more than seven years earlier. He agreed to do so, and his poetic evocation titled "Return" appeared in the* Citizen-Times *on the following Sunday, May 16, 1937. See George W. McCoy, "Asheville and Thomas Wolfe,"* North Carolina Historical Review, *XXX (April, 1953), 200–217.*

Asheville *Daily News,* May 7, 1937

During Wolfe's homecoming week in early May, the newspapers carried
bulletins on his movements. His pronouncements were eagerly recorded.
"Wolfe Home with Avid Views of Life—Writers' Field Only Scratched—
Thomas Wolfe 'Looks Homeward' after Seven Years' Absence; Predicts
Best Books Will Come Out of America in Next 25 Years; Nation Still
Faces Pinnacle of Achievement" was unsigned.

The monotony of everyday existence was broken on Monday by the
return of Thomas Wolfe, writer of *Look Homeward, Angel* and other
best sellers, to the haunts of his youth. He went to New York an awk-
ward mountain youth, so to speak, but for over seven years he looked
the big city squarely in the eye unabashed. He was one of the com-
paratively few who was not ground down by the relentless battering
of urban existence. Something of the vigor of his natural habitat sus-
tained him. He won fame. The sophisticated public proclaimed his
genius and he has come back to Asheville one of the ranking fiction
writers of our day. He is spending the week with his mother, Mrs.
Julia Wolfe, at 48 Spruce Street. He was given a hearty reception by
many of his friends at the American Business Club Tuesday.

After a steady round of calls greeting boyhood friends, Mr. Wolfe
opened his mind for over an hour Tuesday evening to *The Daily*
News representative. He preferred not to discuss local affairs, but
said he had come home to brush up on what had transpired here
since his departure during the boom days of 1929.

As to world problems, he had much to say. Neither communism
nor fascism holds the key to the world's happiness, the writer stated.
His faith is pinned to democracy. However imperfect it may now be,
it holds a richer promise than any other theory evolved.

Asked whether he thought our civilization might give way to a re-
currence of the Middle Ages, he admits that the war in Spain, spread
of the dictator conception through Europe, and other disturbing

signs are causes for grave concern. After spending last summer in Germany, Mr. Wolfe decided, all things considered, that America offered infinitely more. He cited the opinion of a scientific authority that the first 30 years of the present century were the bloodiest in history with the World War and lesser conflicts. No period in the Middle Ages could touch it in human destruction.

Mr. Wolfe sees in the failure of youth to learn from the experience of their elders a waste in human energy and deterrent to progress. The child instinctively must learn at first hand through personal experience with life. He commented, "It is an agonizing thing that human advancement is so slow. Despite lessons learned from the boom and depression, I found people anticipating another boom eagerly.

"Another world war is probable," Mr. Wolfe said. "I was 13 years old when the conflict broke out in 1914. I remember a preparedness debate in which I took part at the Roberts school here. People have learned caution, which will delay the starting of another holocaust. I wrote a story of my observations in the *New Republic* which would make it difficult for me to return to Germany.

"There is a tide flowing about us in this world that is carrying us along to higher things. We cannot define the estuaries and currents of this tide, but in late years I have found a deep conscience in the hearts of men that I didn't recognize before.

"I came away with the profoundest respect and admiration for the German people, but I feel that they are betrayed by false leadership. The German nation is going directly against this tide of progress. Our democratic idea has sometimes been perverted by selfish groups of people, but I think it is the best conception of government we have to live by.

"I saw a certain perfection and finish in European life that we do not have here. However, there is a poisonous atmosphere of hatred. I finally wanted to come back home. I felt that although we lacked this polish, we still had space to move around and develop in. America's hope is not destroyed. Her destiny is real and not a fantastic dream. It is yet to be achieved."

Pacing the floor in deep thought, the author of *Look Homeward,*

Angel continued, "We may be due for a relapse in our civilization, but we cannot go back to former times a hundred years ago and decentralize things, as Gilbert Chesterton would have us do. There may be periods of world chaos, but inventions and the closer linking of the continents will prevent another Middle Ages coming upon us. We have not yet reached the point where America will decay.

"People will tell us that pioneering is at an end in our country, but you can feel that we have not yet attained our destiny. I grew up with the idea that America was vast and illimitable and that we could never be milked dry. The bitter reality has dawned in recent years through floods, dust storms, and erosion that we must pioneer in a new constructive way. We must conserve our resources wisely and think for the welfare of our posterity."

Turning to literature, Mr. Wolfe remarked that people will say, "'No one can really write a book about New York.' Might I ask why? The answer is, 'It is too big.' I don't think I will spend the rest of my life in New York. I find myself wanting to get out. I find that country people have more rugged character and upstanding traits. I used to be chiefly interested in books. Now I am attracted by people. The essential reality of human experience is as alive in the city as in the country.

"We have not even scratched the surface in quality writing. Plots are not running low, as many suppose. Some of the best books will come out of America in the next 25 years. We must try to see America as a whole in spite of its vastness.

"In one typical magazine running an article of mine, I found three stories dealing with fashionable New York night life, three stories of New York and Hollywood divorce life, one story of gangsters and kidnapers, one condensed novel with the divorce and alimony racket theme uppermost. I read these stories over to find out what social and economic figures these characters were. The nearest they came to the life of the average man was the story on the divorce and alimony racket. This magazine has 3,000,000 circulation and is read by at least 15 million people monthly.

"The ages of heroes and heroines averaged between 25 and 35

years. The men were generally wealthy with private yachts and
planes. The women generally possessed wealth and great beauty.
The reader was told that these characters were engineers and lawyers, but were not informed what they engineered or lawed about.

"There are a tremendous number of publishers of books and magazines. The paucity of plots is not due to inspiration being depleted,
but to the demands of readers. Authors are caught in the maelstrom
of demand for that sort of thing. Just this week I talked with a man
in Yancey County who gave me a firsthand description of the battle of
Chickamauga. It was an eyewitness account and would fit into a clas-
sic, but the average magazine would not take it. I do not expect to
run dry of material. I hope I can control and shape it in such a way as
to intrigue the reader.

"Some New York people have an economic or political axe to grind
and writers tend to carry forward the propaganda. Tolstoi ploughed
a deeper furrow and struck a harder blow for his political purposes
by keeping the propaganda element in the background."

Mr. Wolfe talked before the American Business Club Tuesday.

Charlotte *Observer*, October 3, 1937

As promised, Wolfe returned to Asheville in July and August, occupying a cabin at nearby Oteen. Toward the end of August Gertrude S. Carraway took a combined pleasure and feature-writing trip from her home in coastal North Carolina to the western North Carolina mountains. She had long admired the books written by her fellow Tar Heel and in Asheville went to see the Wolfe home, where, "unexpectedly and luckily," she wrote to Richard Walser, September 4, 1982, "I ran into Tom's mother. Kindly she showed me all around and talked a great deal about Tom, whom I had known many years before when he was a student at Chapel Hill. She told me that Tom had been at Oteen for two months and was coming to see her that night. I jumped at the news and, probably through Mrs. Wolfe, I got in touch with Tom and asked him to meet me for an interview. He agreed, and we met that very evening about eight o'clock at the George Vanderbilt Hotel. We sat together on a sofa in the hotel lobby and talked at length. His voice was clear and distinct. He was cordial, courteous, kindly and helpful, not only answering my questions but also adding much additional information. He was very modest and apparently glad to have a chance to reminisce.

"Evidently weary of 'wandering,' he seemed chiefly happy to be back 'home' in the mountains of his native region. There, he said, he would seek a deeper spirituality and power for his character and his work, expecting that his future writing would be the best of his career."

For several weeks, Carraway held on to her notes, then wrote several variations of the interview to appear in North Carolina newspapers on the morning of Wolfe's birthday. The following was titled "Thomas Wolfe, 37 Today, Plans Early Return to Native Mountains to Live—North Carolina's Famous Novelist Is Coming Home—Asheville Young Man, Maturing as Artist, Is Gaining Calmer Outlook upon Life." For another version see State *magazine (Raleigh), October 30, 1937.*

Appropriate for the occasion of his thirty-seventh birthday anniversary today is the news that Thomas Wolfe, one of the most brilliant and prominent young novelists in America, has decided to move back permanently to his native western North Carolina.

For two months this summer he resided in a small cabin near Oteen, and found such inspiration for his work among his beloved Blue Ridge, with such a cordial welcome from the citizens of that section, that he has made up his mind definitely to settle down again in the Old North State.

This was the first season he had returned to North Carolina in eight years, since publication of his first novel, *Look Homeward, Angel*, in October, 1929, when he was twenty-nine years old. The book drew an immediate storm of protests from his native Asheville, which was depicted in the volume as the provincial "Altamont."

Some letters sent to him even threatened to murder him if he should ever dare return home. Other anonymous missives heaped insults and abuse on him. He was denounced from Asheville pulpits, in clubs and on streets. The happiness that Wolfe had experienced from the success of his first book elsewhere was thus ruined by its bitter reception in his hometown.

But now that "Tom" has attained fame abroad, he is being welcomed back to western Carolina with open arms. The old anger has evidently been forgotten in the new pride with which "The Land of the Sky" is now claiming the author as its native son. It is quite apparent that he is immensely pleased at the warm reception and constant attention given him. Years ago he wanted to "escape" from his homeland and he drafted a course of solitude and travel. But now, after the "fury, hunger and all of the wandering in a young man's life," he is delighted to feel at home again.

"To find one's self, the Bible tells us, one must lose himself," he said earnestly at Asheville recently in one of his rare interviews, calling his recent decision a great turning point in his entire life. "And, to find one's country, one must leave it. I love to travel, and for years I wandered through Europe and America. Then I became terribly homesick. I missed the magic of our mountains here. And I love the people of my State. Now that I'm back here, I intend to remain." Accordingly, he expects to close his New York apartment for good and take up a permanent residence in western Carolina—somewhere he can continue his work. Meanwhile, he is visiting literary friends a few weeks in Tennessee and Virginia.

Two years ago he wrote: "The life of the artist at any epoch of man's history has not been an easy one. And here in America it may be the hardest life that man has ever known. Here must we who have no more than what we have, who know no more than what we know, are no more than what we are, find our America. Here, at this present hour and moment of my life, I seek for mine."

Now he is finding his America and himself in his own native region. As he said of Eugene Gant, in his autobiographical fiction, so he might have referred directly to himself: "He was hillborn. His sick heart lifted in the haunting eternity of the hills. . . . Whatever we can do or say must be forever hillbound."

So he hopes from now on to accomplish better results in his literary efforts. He wants to make his literary style more coherent, poetic, spiritual. Though he knows his limitations, he has a calmer assurance as to his capacities, "with less confusion, waste and useless torment."

His first novel, *Look Homeward, Angel*, with the sub-caption, *A Story of the Buried Life*, was described by him as "a story of sweat and pain and despair and partial achievement." Printed over five years later, his second book, *Of Time and the River*, sub-captioned *A Legend of Man's Hunger in His Youth*, was begun in a "whirling vortex and creative chaos." Meanwhile he had written almost two million words. Today he has more definite objectives and more self-confidence for his future writings. In the past few weeks his stories have appeared in three national magazines.

He is finding the long-sought peace and contentment that he believes will be conducive to better writing. Near the government hospital at Oteen where ex-service men regain physical health and vigor, he has taken a new lease on life and labor, with a new mental outlook and spiritual regeneration. Fundamentally spiritual-minded, he is beginning to understand that he is at heart deeply religious and has a special mission in the world.

Eugene Gant, "at seventeen, as a sophomore, triumphantly denied God." The other day, however, Thomas Wolfe declared seriously,
in viewing himself as a poet and artist: "Every artist has a religion.
William Butler Yeats said that man is nothing until his life is united
to an image. Why do I want to work and write? I believe there is
something in one's self that should come out bigger than self. If a
person has a talent, it is wrong not to develop and improve it for the
benefit of mankind. The soul of an artist must express divine love
and ideal beauty in corporeal form. Love is a divine motive power for
real religion."

Hence, after "brutal struggles, pain and ugliness of life," Wolfe is
acquiring a new philosophy in the quiet of his hills. As he explains it,
"Out of man's coarse earth the finer flowers of his spirit sometimes
grow." His new creed has no denominational basis. To him religion
does not mean theory or dogma, but constitutes a vital part of everyday life.

Although he is still convinced that authors must use their own experiences to create anything of substantial value, he now admits that
like other young writers he may have confused "the limits between
actuality and reality" and may have adapted data from life "too
naked and direct for the purpose of a work of art" in describing his
first novel.

He insisted that the book was "a fiction" that he "meditated no
man's portrait" but he confesses that he portrayed various incidents
and characters directly from memory with such "naked intensity of
spirit" that though it was "not true to fact, it was true to the general
experience of the town I came from and I hope, of course, to the general experience of all men living."

During his college days at the University of North Carolina he asserted that literary materials should be drawn from real life. In
proof of this is the foreword to his first one-act play, "The Return of
Buck Gavin," in which he acted as a member of the original Carolina
Playmakers class: "It is a fallacy of the young writer to picture the
dramatic as unusual and remote. . . . It is happening daily in our

lives. . . . True drama is characterized by a certain all-inclusive por-
traiture which, I take it, may be called reality."

Having learned lessons from his first novel, however, and happy
that his fellow citizens are overlooking his early indiscretion along
this line, Mr. Wolfe said recently in Asheville that the new book on
which he is now working for publication will contain "less identifica-
tion and more generalization."

It will be a "historical but modern" novel, about "an innocent
man." Starting out from his home in North Carolina, again to be
called "Catawba," the hero will "go places," somewhat similar in
style to *Gulliver's Travels*. The narrative will be fictional in tone and
spiritual in purpose, and the author promises that it will be more
"humorous" than any of his previous brain children. All of which also
goes to show that Tom Wolfe is "growing up."

In Asheville he admitted that he had changed more in the past
eight years than had North Carolina. Of course, he found new buildings, new highways, new streets in his town and State; but on the
whole there were no real changes here, unless there is a deeper
sense of values brought about by the Depression. He praised this
feature. "We don't want any more booms," he declared. He hopes
that the Depression will have the further effect of bringing about a
spiritual renaissance.

As he spoke with his characteristic rush of words, the same old
vitality and zest were evident in his rich, throaty voice; his piercing,
dark eyes; and his magnetic, dynamic personality. Still an enormous,
overgrown youth, he towers six feet in height and weighs 245 pounds.
His long black, curly hair is still unruly. In his strong, shapely hands,
his tan felt hat was crumpled a hundred ways with his same old nervous intensity. But his former "fury and despair" seem replaced by a
new inner repose and optimism.

One of the main reasons why he is glad to be moving back to North
Carolina is his love of walking. He likes to hike along mountain trails.
"You can't take such swift walks and get such fresh air on city pave-
ments," he asserts.

During his youth he read voraciously in his desire to cram all knowledge in his brain. Now he has so little time left over from his writing that he does not read so much. He seldom goes to movies, but does like the newsreel theaters. Baseball is his favorite outdoor sport.

Every day at Oteen he tried to work from 11 o'clock in the morning to 6 o'clock at night, stopping only to eat a sandwich for lunch. "It's really hard work to write," he declared. "But it is easy to find subjects. When people ask me, as they often do, where I get my materials, I reply, 'Just look around you.'"

A main recreation he used to get in New York was going to the large railroad stations and watching throngs of people surging through the buildings. People form one of his chief studies, pleasures, and inspirations. In North Carolina he hopes to renew all the acquaintances of his youth and make many more friends. For from now on, his native state will be his "home."

But it was not to be. For contrary to the impression he gave Gertrude Carraway, he had discovered that family and friends demanded time he needed for writing. A day or so after the interview, Wolfe slipped away from Asheville never to return.

Though she continued to write, Gertrude S. Carraway resigned from a regular job on her hometown newspaper in New Bern just before her trip to Asheville in 1937.

In 1953 she was elected president general of the Daughters of the American Revolution and resided in Washington. In 1956 she became director of the Tryon Palace Restoration in New Bern.

Roanoke *World-News,* September 11, 1937

On his way north, Wolfe took in reverse the route of the previous spring. He first stopped in Bristol, then spent an evening with Sherwood Anderson in Marion, and proceeded on to Roanoke. His interview by Harold Hayes was titled "Wolfe Plans Novel Patterned after Swift's Famous Satire—Noted Writer of Fiction, Visitor Here, Evinces Many Interests."

An American *Gulliver's Travels* is in the making.

Thomas Wolfe, prominent novelist who is a guest at Hotel Patrick Henry, reported last night that he was planning a new novel patterned somewhat after the famous satire by Jonathan Swift. His hero, he indicated, will visit various spots typical of the American scene and an observant reader should recognize many of the places and happenings to be portrayed.

Mr. Wolfe, himself, calls to mind the "Man Mountain," Gulliver, who visited the land of Lilliput. He is so tall that you fear for his head as he walks under an electric fan hanging from the ceiling. He greets you, though, with all the good nature which Gulliver displayed toward the tiny Lilliputians, and soon you are completely at ease.

The famous novelist arrived in Roanoke Thursday en route from Asheville, N.C., his former home, to New York City. On the way here, he stopped at Marion to visit Sherwood Anderson, another well-known writer. Mr. Wolfe is the author of *Look Homeward, Angel, Of Time and the River,* both novels, and a number of short stories. One of his stories appears in the current issue of *The Saturday Evening Post,* and another is scheduled for publication in the November number of *Red Book.*

"My father was a stonecutter," mused Mr. Wolfe, as he sat on his bed at the hotel. "He had to have rocks from which to hew his product. My experiences are to me what stones were to him. They are material from which I carve my stories."

With this statement, you realize that he is completely lacking in the pseudosophistication that parades itself so ostentatiously in intelligent circles today. His manner is one of simplicity and straightforwardness, and he never tries to hide his meaning behind a subterfuge of obscure and fanciful words. He pours forth his thoughts with a directness which is gripping, and his very simplicity drives home to you the complex thoughts he has in his mind.

"All writing is, to a certain extent, autobiographical," continued Mr. Wolfe.

He explained that one does not have to give a literal account of things he has experienced or observed but that he is quite likely to write about things which have come within the range of his experience.

"If I am writing about a horse thief who lives in Spartanburg," he said, "I don't have to give his name and street address. For literary purposes, I could just as easily have him living in Paducah, Ky., and could avoid the embarrassments which follow a too literal version of his deeds."

If a work is to have literary merit it must not be concerned with private likes or dislikes but it must deal with life on a higher scale, he said. The writer may approach his story with certain definite persons in mind, he must tell a tale which will arouse the interest of his readers in his characters as people, he continued.

Mr. Wolfe writes in longhand in what he describes as a "torrential manner." When thoughts and moods grip him, he pours them out on paper just as they seethe within him, he said. Afterwards he revises his manuscripts, in some cases as many as a dozen times, and then he has them typed.

"I wonder if it would be very hard to learn typing?" he asked suddenly.

The absorbing interest which Mr. Wolfe shows in every phase of life partially explains his success as a novelist. He may be watching a burlesque show at a carnival, discussing social conditions over a schooner of beer, or looking at deserted streets after midnight, and perhaps all of these will appear later in some book he is to write. Never at any time, though, does he give you the impression that he is simply out looking for copy; instead, you feel that anything he ever writes about them will arise from an intense and burning interest in them—an interest which is the thing to be cultivated for its own sake and only secondarily because it can be translated into stories which are saleable.

Two Wolfe enthusiasts, Jay Hall and Dayton Kohler, drove to Roanoke from Blacksburg to see him. Wolfe invited them and their wives to dinner, saying, "I got a check cashed today, so we'll make this a good party." Though he planned to give up his apartment in New York, he said he would not be moving to Asheville. "People just wouldn't let him alone down there." He thought "perhaps he could find the quiet he needed for his new book in one of the little towns near York Springs. . . . Yes, Pennsylvania might be the place." See Dayton Kohler, "Thomas Wolfe: Of Time and Legend," Commonwealth: The Magazine for Pennsylvania, *II (April, 1948), 23–27.*

After Roanoke, he went to Baltimore and was back in New York for his thirty-seventh birthday.

Purdue *Exponent*, May 20, 1938

Fatigued after months of steady work in his suite at the Hotel Chelsea in New York and ready for a vacation, Wolfe eagerly accepted an invitation from the Department of English at Purdue University to be the speaker at a banquet. He wrote out a sixty-three-page speech "just for the sake of getting it objectively stated," knowing it was far too long to be read at a dinner. He then packed up his manuscripts, turned over a sizable portion of them to his new editor Edward Aswell, and took a train westward. See William Braswell and Leslie A. Field (eds.), Thomas Wolfe's Purdue Speech: "Writing and Living" *(Purdue University Studies, 1964).*

In the Exponent *(a Purdue University campus publication) was a brief interview by K. C. Houston headed "Beauty, Size of Campus Impress Visiting Speaker."*

Smoking endless cigarettes and pacing back and forth—too full of energy to remain seated—as he talked, Literary Banquet Speaker Thomas Wolfe, about six feet six inches tall, with black curly hair, and wearing glasses, expressed his desire "to talk from the work shop," as he was interviewed yesterday afternoon.

"I worked right up to the minute I got here, so I am going to talk right from my shop," he added, explaining that by "my shop" he meant his personal qualification and equipment as a writer.

This is the first time he has had an opportunity to visit Purdue, he explained, and said he was much impressed by the beauty and largeness of the campus. "I think this country around here is beautiful. It's so different from where I come from," he said, adding that he had been born in the mountains of North Carolina.

"As a writer, I wish I knew a lot more about engineering," Wolfe divulged. A writer can improve his work greatly through knowledge of such subjects as engineering, medicine, and other sciences, he added.

After working hard for seven months, Thomas Wolfe decided to take a few weeks' vacation in the West before returning to work on a two-million-word book he is writing. "I'll have to go back to New York soon," he concluded.

Kenneth C. Houston, former Purdue student, a civil engineer, now lives in Arlington, Virginia.

Printed alongside the interview was an unsigned news story, "Writers Have Their Place in World, Says T. Wolfe—Professors Creek, Cummings Announce Winners in Campus Short Story, Poem, Essay, Literary Contests." The names of the many contestants have been omitted in the following account. The reporter failed to mention that Wolfe used no notes in making his address.

Writers have a definite place in the world, Thomas Wolfe, speaker at the annual Literary Banquet, told approximately 300 people, mostly faculty and townspeople, last night in the Union ballroom. A self-titled poor speaker, Wolfe held the attention of the audience by his intense sincerity.

"I think a writer has a place in the world, just the same as an engineer, business man, or lawyer," said the tall novelist, who stood a head over President E. C. Elliott, toastmaster for the dinner. "People can't quite get it into their heads that a writer has to write," complained Wolfe.

"Writing is a business just the same as any other vocation," he said. "You have to use what you've got; you can't use what you haven't got. My father got calluses on his hands from his occupation of stone cutting, and I get calluses on my hand from writing with a pencil."

After Wolfe's speech, winners in the various literary contests on the campus were announced by Profs. H. L. Creek and F. A. Cummings, of the University English department.

Wolfe's Purdue speech was a great success. His three hundred faculty and student listeners were as affected by how he spoke as by what he said. *He had a wonderful time in Lafayette, completely at ease with his newfound friends, enjoying the many receptions and parties in his honor.*

When the time came for his departure he talked some of them into coming along with him for a weekend in Chicago. One of those in Wolfe's party was William Braswell of Purdue's English Department, who wrote about that fun-filled weekend in an article that appeared in College English, I *(October, 1939), and was later reprinted in Richard Walser (ed.),* The Enigma of Thomas Wolfe *(Cambridge, Mass., 1953), and William Braswell and Leslie A. Field (eds.),* Thomas Wolfe's Purdue Speech: "Writing and Living" *(Purdue University Studies, 1964).*

Braswell recalled the Friday night ride from Lafayette to Chicago, with Wolfe in rare good humor, and his repeated renditions of "Heigh Ho, Heigh Ho," from Snow White and the Seven Dwarfs. *He also recounted some of Wolfe's antics in Chicago—feeding several boxes of Cracker Jacks to the polar bears in Brookfield Zoo, tramping gleefully across the mattress on his bed at the Auditorium Hotel, his delight at winning a twenty-five-cent bet when the New York Yankees whipped the Chicago White Sox, and his insisting that everyone have German pancakes for dessert at the Red Star Inn.*

Wolfe talked constantly about his intention to go to the Northwest after visiting in Colorado but promised to stop in Chicago for another party on his way back East. He said good-bye to his Purdue friends, boarded the Burlington Zephyr, and headed on to Denver.

Denver *Post*, May 25, 1938

Wolfe's high spirits during the Chicago weekend, coupled with the excite-
ment he always felt when he was embarking upon a new experience,
were apparent upon his arrival in Denver. He immediately fell in with
Thomas Hornsby Ferril and other good friends he had met three years
before at the Boulder Writers' Conference. They were genuinely happy to
be with him again and did everything they could to show him a good
time. Wolfe enjoyed himself so much that the intended one-day visit to
Denver extended to a week.

Shortly after his arrival an interview by Frances Wayne appeared
under the title "T. C. Wolfe, 'Wordiest Author,' Pays Visit to Denver on
Whim—Urges Formation of Political Party by Young Men and Women
Fresh from Nation's Schools, Colleges and Universities."

There was no sound of a political bee buzzing in the tousled black
hair of Thomas E. Wolfe [*sic*], the author, when he said, "There must
be room in these United States for a political party composed of
young men and women who, fresh from schools, colleges and universities, have learned what America means and what has been the cost
of production."

Several days ago Wolfe made a speech at Purdue University and
had reached Chicago on his way to somewhere else when of a sudden, he was seized with a desire to come back to Denver, "one of the
finest cities in this world."

So off the Burlington Zephyr he stepped Wednesday morning,
and, with his huge figure filling a window of his room on the eighth
floor of the Brown Palace Hotel, he talked of this and that and many
things concerning this country.

One refers to this North Carolinian, now 37, as the "wordiest of
modern authors," remembering the "heft" of his novels. At the same
time, however, comes recollection that Wolfe has a habit of balancing
words with ideas—live, imagination-firing ideas.

"But you haven't seen anything yet," he said, with a chuckle, "for just before coming west I placed the first million words of my new story of America in the hands of the publisher. Now let him suffer a while!"

When Wolfe was graduated from Harvard University he was convinced that Paris was the place for the rare and special young fellow who wants to put the world on its ear at a later date.

"What a fool!" he said, when recalling his life with the Bohemians on the Seine. "It didn't take me long to find out my mistake. Fancy going to Paris with all America, and the best of it here in the west, stretching all around one!

"I realized then and now that one must see and meet life in terms of people—the more real they are, the better. Here and where I came from is the place to find them. I came down and out of my ivory tower.

"Once upon a time not so long ago, I thought a man who wanted to do something really worth-while should keep away from and out of politics. Try to keep politics away from you! It can't be done. Not these days! That is why I feel that every loyal American-loving young man and woman should go into politics, preferably, if possible, under their own party banner.

"If the two old parties, Democratic and Republican, have outlived their usefulness, as it is asserted they have, there are enough of us to form a new one.

"I came from Chicago to Denver. I'm too long for the sleeping car accommodations, but not too long to curl up and look out the window and watch the country slip by. As I watched, I visualized what this west had been—and not a century ago—and what it is. I thought of the superb initiative, of the courage, almost out of human bounds, required to take over the desert and the mountains. I thought of the men and women who had pioneered. I thought of the initiative and faith necessary to build the railroads, of the epitome of comfort created for travelers like myself in these new trains and then I came to the conclusion that none of us, born and raised in America, has a right to keep aloof from what concerns its welfare."

Feeling deeply as he does regarding America, Wolfe should write an epic story regarding its program from 1793 to the present. He'll use words—millions of them—to tell the story.

"But that's my custom," he said. "Sometimes, when packing up my manuscripts for delivery to the publisher I wish I had had newspaper training which teaches one to abridge in a sentence a whole event, and if people want to read on after the headline or first paragraph, that is their affair."

The author will be in Denver a day or two, meeting friends, then will go to Yellowstone Park and into Oregon, where some more genuine Americans live and remember because they heard at first hand how their ancestors trekked across the land to make new homes and create an empire.

Through four decades as one of the distinctive figures in western journalism, Frances Wayne became a familiar and looked-for name to many thousands of Denver Post *readers. She died in July, 1951, at the age of eighty-one.*

In a second interview, "The Prodigious Mr. Wolfe Takes a Moment Off—Noted Writer Says Work Is Artist's Food and Drink," by Miriam Wise, in the Rocky Mountain News, *May 26, 1938, Wolfe complained that being on vacation and away from his rigid writing schedule, he generated energy at such a rate that sleep was out of the question. "But I want to rest," he exclaimed excitedly. "I want to rest and see the country. I love Denver—it is a beautiful city, and it is full of vitality and newness. People are doing things here. They have good times—and they accomplish things, too."*

The theme of work and its many values monopolized his thoughts, and he wanted to talk about it. He told his interviewer that work was "the sensitive person's salvation and as important as food and drink to the artist. At 23, when I was a student at Harvard, I sat and talked about beauty and art. At that age an artist says to himself: 'Life is your enemy. Stay away from it. Avoid reality. Avoid the people who don't speak your language.' At 37, I honestly believe that to be an artist, one must be a man of life. And the thing that puts you close to life is work.

"Work itself is a dignified experience," said he. "It is important that young people understand this. When you work, you begin to get respect for other people. You stop sneering at the people who don't understand you, and you begin to understand them.

"When you work and work hard, the whole field of your objectivity widens, and your personal problems grow smaller in proportion."

Seattle *Post-Intelligencer,* June 17, 1938

After leaving Denver with brief stopovers in Cheyenne and Boise to soak up the scenery, Wolfe arrived in Portland on Tuesday, June 8, 1938. After checking in at the University Club, he immediately got in touch with writer Stewart Holbrook, who took him to the J. K. Gill Company to meet several people in the book department. Warren Wright, the manager, was taken with Wolfe and invited him, along with other guests, to a house party lasting several days at his summer cabin on the Washougal River near Camas. It was there that Wolfe met a number of Portland writers.

During that week in Portland he was contacted by David W. Hazen, who wanted to interview him for the Oregonian. *Wolfe agreed, and when Hazen brought him to the newspaper offices for a picture, he was introduced to Sunday section editor Edward M. Miller. Miller had never read any of Wolfe's books and knew very little about him but was pleased to learn that he was from Asheville, only about twenty miles from Mrs. Miller's birthplace. Knowing she would be delighted to meet someone from her "neck of the woods," Miller promptly invited Wolfe to their home for dinner.*

During the course of the evening Miller told Wolfe about a trip he was planning with his friend T. Raymond Conway, manager of the Oregon State Motor Association. The trip, sponsored by Conway's organization and Miller's newspaper, had an exhausting itinerary that involved traveling an average of 350 miles a day through Oregon, California, Arizona, Utah, Idaho, Wyoming, Montana, and Washington. The purpose was to prove that the eleven national parks spread along the Cascade, Sierra Nevada, and Rocky Mountain ranges could be visited in the course of an average two-week vacation. Miller invited Wolfe to join him and Conway on the trip. Although Wolfe was eager to return to New York and begin work with Edward Aswell on his huge manuscript, he agreed to go along. See Edward M. Miller, "The Western Journey: Prelude and Aftermath," Thomas Wolfe Newsletter, *I (Spring, 1977), 20–21, later reprinted in a slightly altered form in Brian F. Berger,* Thomas Wolfe: The Final Journey *(West Linn, Ore., 1984).*

*On June 15 he wrote Elizabeth Nowell that he was planning "on what
promises to be one of the most remarkable trips of my life. It means I'll
be away about two weeks longer than I intended, but it is the chance of a
lifetime and after long battlings with my conscience, I have decided I'd
be foolish not to take it. . . . I've seen wonderful things and met every
kind of person—doctors, lawyers, lumberjacks, etc.—and when I get
through with this I'll have a whole wad of glorious material. . . . When I
get through I shall really have seen America (except Texas)."*

*In a postcard written on June 16, Wolfe reported to his mother that he
was unable to locate any of the Westall relatives in Oregon. He then
planned a short trip to Seattle in hopes of finding some kin there. It was,
after all, the real reason for visiting the Northwest.*

*Wolfe arrived in Seattle on Wednesday, June 15, settled in at the New
Washington Hotel, and immediately telephoned James Stevens to arrange a get-together. Stewart Holbrook had written to Stevens about
Wolfe's impending visit and had suggested that he and Wolfe meet. In ad-
dition to being the public relations officer of the West Coast Lumbermen's
Association, Stevens was well known for his Paul Bunyan stories and
tales of lumbering in the Northwest. James and Theresa Stevens had
dinner with Wolfe the next evening at his hotel, and on the following day
Stevens took Wolfe across Puget Sound to Port Townsend on the Olympic
peninsula for a tour of logging and milling operations. Although Wolfe
spent a good deal of time with the Stevenses at their home, where he met
many of those active in the literary and artistic life of the city, he also
managed to locate and visit with some of his mother's Westall relatives in
the area. See V. L. O. Chettick, "Tom Wolfe's Farthest West," Southwest
Review, XLVIII (Spring, 1963), 95.*

*While in Seattle Wolfe was interviewed by Robert Berman of the Seattle
Post-Intelligencer. Accompanying the interview, "Author Wolfe Visits
Seattle; He's Just as Big as His Books—6-Foot 7-Inch Novelist Here" was
a photograph by Ken Harris of Wolfe towering over Stevens, both men
smiling broadly and shaking hands.*

Seattle played host yesterday to a real literary giant.

He is Thomas Clayton Wolfe, who has a double claim to the title.
Not only does he write—and sell—novels longer than *Anthony Ad-*

verse or *Gone with the Wind,* but, physically, he's just as big as his books. He's six feet seven in height, and broad in proportion.

"I used to be sensitive about my size," he remarked last night in his room at the New Washington Hotel. "But I'm not any more—except when I try to get into a Pullman berth."

He was chatting with Jim Stevens, the Seattle author, who felt right at home, because his favorite character is Paul Bunyan, who was a little—but not much—bigger than Wolfe.

Wolfe explained that he is taking a vacation after finishing a rough draft of his latest novel, tentatively called *The Web and the Rock,* which runs into no less than two million words. And every word of it was written by hand.

"I never learned to use a typewriter," Wolfe said apologetically, "so it takes me quite a time. But I work hard when I'm at it—eight or nine hours a day. I turn out pretty close to a million words a year.

"Of course, all of that doesn't get into print. I do a lot of revising and rewriting. But I seem to have to get it all out of me first."

His first best seller, *Look Homeward, Angel,* ran a mere quarter of a million words in the finished product. But his *Of Time and the River* came to seven hundred thousand.

Incidentally, his works have been published in German, but he hasn't benefited much from that because of the Nazi ban on sending money out of Germany.

"I have 5,000 marks coming to me in Germany right now," he observed. "But I can't get it unless I go there, and I'd have to spend it all before I left the country. I found that was pretty unprofitable when I did it in 1936. I collected 2,000 marks, but I spent so much more that I had to send home for money.

"It was worth it, though, because I saw the University of Washington crew win its race [at the 1936 Olympics in Berlin]—and that's a sight I'll never forget."

Wolfe said his father was a stonecutter and his mother has never been able to get used to the idea that he doesn't follow the same calling.

"I remember once when I sold a story to the *Saturday Evening*

Post," he said. "Mother asked me if I got paid for that sort of thing. When I told her I did she said I certainly was lucky, because all the rest of my folks had to work for a living."

This is Wolfe's first visit to the Northwest and he expressed himself as delighted with the free-and-easy characteristics of the people he is meeting.

"I've spent a lot of time in Europe," he said, "and I'm just beginning to realize how much I've been missing in not seeing my own country."

Wolfe returned to Portland late Saturday, June 18, with plenty of time to get ready for the exciting trip around the western national parks circuit. On Monday morning the group left the University Club at 8:15 sharp. It was a "fair day, bright sunlight, no cloud in the sky—Went South by East through farmlands of upper Willamette and around base of Mount Hood which was glowing in brilliant sun." The Oregon State Motor Association provided the car, a white Ford displaying the AAA insignia. Conway and Miller took turns at the wheel every hundred miles. Wolfe, who had never learned to drive, relaxed in a new gabardine suit, stretched his huge body along the back seat, and drank in the sights. See Thomas Wolfe, A Western Journal *(Pittsburgh, 1951), 3.*

Portland *Sunday Oregonian,* July 3, 1938

The national parks trip of more than forty-five hundred miles in thirteen days ended at Mount Rainier on July 2. Wolfe, Conway, and Miller drove into Olympia, where they had a final lunch together at a seafood restaurant. After a sentimental parting, Miller and Conway drove back to Portland and Wolfe boarded a bus in the late afternoon for a return visit to Seattle. There he was planning to keep a dinner date with the Stevenses and rest for a few days, hoping to catch up on his sleep. He also wanted to polish some rough notes he had taken during the trip.

Again checking in at the New Washington Hotel late in the afternoon of July 2, he was pleased to find waiting for him a wire from Edward Aswell, who had been reading the huge manuscript Wolfe had deposited with him back in May. "Dear Tom," the wire said, "Your new book is magnificent in scope and design, with some of the best writing you have ever done. I am still absorbing it, confident that when you finish you will have written your greatest novel so far. Hope you come back full of health and new visions."

In a letter to Elizabeth Nowell July 3, Wolfe reported that his parks trip was "wonderful and terrific" and that he was "thinking of buying some firecrackers and spending to-morrow in H.M.'s Canadian town of Victoria, B.C."

On the day that Wolfe wrote this last letter to Nowell, an interview, "Thomas Wolfe: He Writes 'Em Standing Up—Noted Author Does Work at Night—Novel Rejected First Later Published—Icebox Served as Writing Desk," by David W. Hazen, appeared. Although Wolfe had been interviewed during his first Portland visit, the long newspaper piece with Wolfe talking headlong uninterrupted by questions from Hazen did not appear until almost three weeks later. Accompanying it was a photograph of Wolfe captioned "Thomas Wolfe posed for this photo in The Oregonian office to prove he can write sitting down—when he wants to."

Reprinted by permission of the *Oregonian.*

"I believe a man, even one who is a gentleman, should have a bit of coarseness in him!" Thomas Wolfe, novelist of exalted rank, made the statement. No ifs nor ands nor buts followed. When the "he" gets out of a man's makeup, Wolfe thinks the guy has become a sissy.

Life has been pretty rough with the author of *Look Homeward, Angel* and *Of Time and the River*. He has had to miss many meals because both the cupboard and the pocketbook were bare. The combination has tended to keep him a bachelor, although fortune is getting much more kindly.

Born in Asheville, N.C., October 3, 1900, he was the son of a northern father and a southern mother. A penitentiary caused his father to stay in North Carolina, but we'll get to that a bit later. When Thomas went to college at the University of North Carolina, he decided to become a writer.

But not a word of this did he tell during visits back to Asheville— "You know that in a small community, if you admit you want to be a writer your friends immediately know you have a screw loose," the author announced.

Wolfe said they may have been right at that.

"My father wanted me to be a lawyer—I think I'd made a hell of a lawyer," continued the 6-foot-6 fellow from North Carolina. "He wanted me to take the bachelor of arts course, then take a law course; but I think it's just as well that I didn't because the south has too many lawyers now."

Thomas Wolfe worked on the college paper at U. of N.C. He reported, wrote sports items from football field and fraternity houses, became an editor. But suddenly he decided to write plays. They got by on Chapel Hill. When he received the B.A. there, to Harvard he went to study playwriting and get a master's degree.

"I wrote plays, all right, but didn't get anywhere with them," he confessed at Portland's University Club the other day. "The same objection was raised to my plays as is raised to my books—too long and too many characters. You can get away with it in books, but in plays they demand briefness, conciseness.

"And then the theater is a business concern as well as an art institution, and if you have too many characters it takes more money to produce a play because too many actors are needed."

Finding that Walter Hampden and Otis Skinner and Charles Coburn and other Broadway stars didn't demand his plays, Wolfe managed to get to Paris in the summer of 1926. There he thought he might have better luck with his dramatic efforts. But from the French he received the equivalent to the well-known raspberry.

"Maybe," thought the large young man, "they don't want my plays."

He really had something in that thought. So he started on a new line.

"In Paris that summer I bought an old brown tablet; I still have it, but it's as full of words as a hound dog is full of bites," continued Wolfe, getting into real vocal stride. "The idea of a book had been formulating in my mind, and I put the notes down as they came to me.

"I had taken two very good plays to France, but nothing came of them. I still have them somewhere. Maybe in time the stage will grow up to them. If it ever does, I'll let you know.

"After I had spent several months in Paris—I had a little money when I left Boston—I decided to try England. No, I didn't offer the king my plays. I went to London, and got a room down in Chelsea. It was there I definitely made up my mind to write a book. I didn't know anyone in London at the time—I had a pretty hollow feeling inside of me at that period.

"Here I was, 4000 miles from home, trying to write a book and knowing nothing about how to do it. Right there I learned that writing is hard work. At Harvard, when I was taking that writing course, we sat around and talked about love and art and literature, but there was no stern labor to it.

"I had a very ordinary front room in Wellington Square. The house was rented by an old man who had been a butler in a very flossy family. He was a great character; I haven't used him yet, but I'm going to. He was a real Tory. I have noticed that the people who worked for Tories are a great deal more reactionary than the Tories themselves.

"This old chap could forgive the rich any of their sins, but poor devils had to stay right in the middle of the straight and narrow path."

Thomas Wolfe talked as fast as he could. And all the while he paced back and forth in his room, like the circus lion in his cage just before feeding time. The literary person had to be halted time after time in his torrent of words. Few newspaper men have the penmanship speed of court reporters. It was also terrific wear and tear on the University Club carpet.

"I was there five months," continued Wolfe, after a couple of minutes' rest. "I went out and bought some big ledgers, the biggest ledgers I could find. I figured if I wrote in ledgers I could keep my words together, but if I wrote on scraps of paper, they would get lost. So I started to work with a pencil, and began getting my thoughts on paper.

"I worked at night because the night-time has always excited me. Night-time awakens a more alert chemistry in me. The United States is a sort of night-time country. Down south people will sit up until crack of day just talking about things. At the University of North Carolina we boys would stay up and talk all night just to be doing something.

"I have a theory that some of the greatest writing has been done at night or tells about the doings in the night. I think Mark Twain's finest book is *Life on the Mississippi*, and the best writing in that story is his telling of the nights on the river. If you'll just try to think—I know it's damn hard to try and think while I'm talking here all the time—but if you can, you'll recall that a very large percentage of our best American literature tells of night-time adventures—or authors explain that they did most of their work after dark.

"In London I began writing about 7 o'clock at night and continued until sometime in the morning. When the old woman who kept my room cleaned up appeared, I would eat a bite of breakfast, take a walk sometimes, then go to bed. She was an old Tory, too. When some baron or lord would go broke she would almost weep for him. I would tell her that even though he was broke, he had more than she did, that she shouldn't worry about the hardened old sinner.

"'But they are gentlemen, they can't live this way, we are used to it,' she would say. And my reply was always the same, 'Oh, hell!'"

"After five months of London, I returned to this native land of ours. If you don't think it is good, try five months in London cheap lodgings. I came back with 100,000 words written in the ledgers. This is about the size of a regular novel, but with me it was just an introduction. I got me a garret room down on Eighth Street near Fifth Avenue, in New York. It had good light, that was its one big charm.

"It had been used as a sweat shop. There were things about it that would have made an Astor or Vanderbilt object to living in the place. There was plenty of space, and that is what I always like—maybe it is because I am so big myself I want plenty of room to move around in.

"I stayed in that big garret for six months, working all night long and sleeping part of the day. In New York, where there is so much traffic by day, one can concentrate much better at night. There was no heat at night, I was the only person in the building at night. The front room door was hanging on one hinge, it was as wide open as a bass drum. The old bums from the Bowery used to come in at night, and prowl around on the second and third floors, hunting a place to sleep. I didn't have the heart to run them out on those cold nights, but I was afraid of fire. They smoked sometimes, but we were lucky.

"It was an old four-story house, and I was in the garret. A long time ago—I used to think it was before Stonewall Jackson scared the Yankees so badly—it had been a fine mansion, a wonderful place. You could tell this by the fine stairways that had been left in the house.

"I was there from January to July. When it would begin to get cold after the heat had been turned off, I would put on my best overcoat, and go to it. I was working so hard I didn't think anything other than the north pole would have stopped me.

"By the end of June I had filled up a dozen very large ledgers—but the book was not finished, although I had several hundred thousand words written. In July I went back to central Europe to spend the summer, having gotten a cash fellowship to do some research over there. I was home again in September, and was given a job as an instructor in English at New York University. I worked on the book at night. It was finished, that is, the first draft was finished in the spring of 1928—remember, though, it is just as important to rewrite a book as it is to write it.

"I had worked on it for two years!"

Thomas Wolfe rested a minute. There was water in the room, so he drank some of it. It gave him a fresh start.

"I rewrite a great deal," he admitted, renewing his marathon. "I pour it out. By the time I get ready to write it has to come like Niagara Falls. I have the habit of torrential production. For my first book I wrote more than 500,000 words, but when I submitted it to a publisher it had been reduced to only 350,000 words.

"It was rejected in two weeks. It didn't take them long. The publisher sent back a cute note saying my story was much too long, and that it was autobiographical, that he had published a half dozen novels similar to mine the year before and had lost money on all of them.

"That was a bitter disappointment to me. It made me feel I was just one of those idiots who thinks he can write without having any talent for it. I threw this huge manuscript into the closet, shut the door and tried to forget the darn thing.

"I went to Europe again for the summer, leaving the manuscript behind. In October I was in Munich—beautiful city, isn't it?—when I received a letter from another publisher, who had heard about my manuscript from an agent who was a friend of mine. My friend had gone to the closet, got the manuscript and let the agent look it over. That letter was such good news that I committed it to memory. Do you want to hear it? Well, I'm going to repeat it to you, anyway. It went like this:

"'I have read the manuscript of your novel, and, although I do not know that any publisher could publish it in its present form and at its present length, I do know that no editor could fail to be excited by it. What I should like to know is, when are you returning to the United States so I can see you and talk to you about it?'

"I got back in New York on December 31, 1928. I was broke when I landed. I had only $1.25 to my name. I had a job coming up, starting in February, at the New York University, but, hell, I had to eat before February. I made that $1.25 last me until January 2, then I walked around to see the pleasant publisher. I walked because I didn't have a nickel to pay subway fare.

"We talked it over. He said he wanted it. And he didn't have to coax me for that manuscript either. He advised that I cut it down to 250,000 words, and I told him I would. I talked a lot, but he didn't mention money. It's a terrible thing to talk about money, but, boy, I needed a bit of it. So as I took my hat I said to the nice man, 'I have no money; I'll have a good coaching job in February, but the doctor advises that I eat something before then.'

"'Oh,' says the publisher, 'I'll get you an advance.' Pretty soon he came back waving a check for $500. It looked bigger than the national debt. I walked out into the street holding that check in my hand. I walked up the avenue a long way holding that check. At last I went into a restaurant, still holding the check out in plain sight.

"Listen, Hazen, it wasn't the fact that I had so much money that made me that way, that made me so totally happy, but it was because my confidence had been restored. And I went to work right away cutting out words."

Mr. Wolfe then told the story of how his first book received a name.

"My original title for it was 'O Lost,'" he explained. "But as the book went to press the editors called me in and said my title wouldn't do. It wasn't any good at all, they said. I was asked to submit something else. So I wrote out 12 other titles, any one of which I was willing to father. None clicked. Editors have ideas that authors know nothing about like women thinking about men.

"I had had a story in *Scribner's* several months before that ran under the title, 'An Angel on the Porch.' But originally I had called it, 'Look Homeward, Angel.' So, as we sat talking, one of them recalled this magazine yarn, and he said, 'What did you originally call that magazine story?'

"'Look Homeward, Angel,' I replied.

"'That's it, that's it,' he shouted, 'that's the title for this book.'

"It sold well for a first book and it is still selling. It got my name known as a writer. And it raised a lot of hell in my home town. Critics received it well but they asked, 'What is this man going to do next?' This was a challenge, and boys in North Carolina are taught never to take a dare without fighting. So I had to get down to writing again.

"*Look Homeward, Angel* was published in October, 1929. The next book was *Of Time and the River*. It took less than two years to write. I wrote most of it in a basement apartment facing the alleyway in the Syrian section of Brooklyn. I wrote nearly 4,000,000 words for the first draft of this book. And I wrote the most of it standing up.

"I used the top of an old refrigerator for a table. I decided that I wouldn't throw away the words I didn't use in my new book; I just put them aside to add to books I'm working on now. I took out nearly 500,000 words of the 4,000,000 and used them in *Of Time and the River*. This was published in March, 1935, by Charles Scribner's Sons.

"It has also been published in England, Sweden, Norway and Germany. It had a great success in Germany, but I can't get any money out of there. The French are negotiating for it now, but they say it is so long and can't they bring it out in five volumes? Sure they can if their terms are all right."

Mr. Wolfe said the two books named were written at night, but times have changed the 275-pound giant from North Carolina. Oh, yes, his father was an expert stonecutter, and went to Raleigh, N.C., in 1870 to help build the new penitentiary. He later moved to Asheville, wed Julia Westall, whose father and uncles were Confederate soldiers and mighty proud of it. Mr. Wolfe Sr. had worked in Baltimore for the contractor who had the stonework on the new prison, thus the job.

"Now I write mostly by day," Thomas Wolfe announced. "I have been pouring it out like flowing lava for the last four or five years. I write in longhand, on large sheets of yellow paper, handing them to the girl as I finish them, and she types them. We begin work at 10 A.M. and then go just as long as we can, sometimes to 7:30 P.M.

"Then at night I revise and correct what I have written and try to have the revised copy for her in the morning. This gives me time to get started on a new day's work.

"On days when I really have been going good I have put out 5000 words. But usually I put out about 3000 words a day when I'm working. When I'm working I try to get one good meal a day. I have this meal around 8 or 9 o'clock at night. I often miss lunch, but then it's not a good idea to eat lunch, because it slows you down in the afternoon. My breakfast is a cup of coffee and some orange juice, but when the girl comes before I've had breakfast I just don't have any, because I have to go to work right away.

"What it amounts to is this, Mr. Hazen. I work just as hard as I can while I am working. And for the last few months I've had trouble sleeping at night, because this new book I'm working on keeps buzzing in my head. It will be a long book—in fact, it will be published in four volumes, each one with a separate title, but working into one complete story beginning in 1793 and coming down to 1938.

"The general title of this book will be, I think, *The Web and the Rock*. Now, 'The Rock' is that thing in us that remains and never changes and 'The Web' is that thing that goes back and forth, that changes us and changes our lives—a man is what he is, he is what he came from, but still he goes and comes like the tide."

The novelist had walked and talked a lot. He said thousands more words during the interview than can be put into this article. He was tired, thirsty. But just before we started down to the University Club's buttermilk department Thomas Wolfe said wistfully: "Hazen, I would rather be a poet than anything else in the world, gosh, I sure would."

In a postcard to Elizabeth Nowell, postmarked July 6, Wolfe reported that he had just left Victoria, B.C., and was on his way by ship to Vancouver. He said he would be back in Seattle in a few days and then to work.

"It was on this boat trip to Victoria and Vancouver that Wolfe shared a pint of whisky which he had bought with 'a poor, shivering wretch,' who

*probably had influenza, and from whom Wolfe is believed to have con-
tracted the respiratory infection which finally resulted in his death. By
the afternoon of July 6, Wolfe was seriously ill with high fever, pains in
his lungs, and protracted chills. However, instead of going to a hospital
in Vancouver, he took a train back to Seattle and remained, still desperately ill, in the New Washington Hotel there for five more days. Finally,
on July 11, he was examined by Dr. E. C. Ruge, who found him to have
pneumonia and hospitalized him at Firlawns Sanitarium at Bothell,
Washington. By July 15th, Wolfe seemed to have passed the crisis of his
pneumonia. . . . However, during the period of his convalescence, Wolfe
began to have recurrent fever and other disquieting symptoms. By the
first week of August, Dr. Ruge had him taken to Providence Hospital in
Seattle so that X-rays of his lungs could be made. These revealed an un-
resolved condition of the upper lobe of the right lung, which the X-ray
specialist and Dr. Ruge diagnosed as an old tubercular lesion, but
which other doctors considered to be only the result of his pneumonia.*

    *"Wolfe remained at Providence Hospital until September 4th, by
which time he was suffering from violent headaches and moments of
slight irrationality. On the recommendation of the physicians who had
succeeded Dr. Ruge when Wolfe entered Providence Hospital, Mabel
Wolfe Wheaton, who had come to Seattle to be with Wolfe during his ill-
ness, took him by train to Johns Hopkins Hospital in Baltimore. There,
on September 12, Dr. Walter E. Dandy performed an exploratory opera-
tion on his brain. It was found that germs of tuberculosis, released from
an old lesion on Wolfe's lung by his recent pneumonia, had entered his
blood stream and been carried to his brain. He died of cerebral infection
three days later, on September 15, 1938." See Elizabeth Nowell (ed.),* The
Letters of Thomas Wolfe *(New York, 1956), 776–77.*

Carolina Magazine, October, 1938

The following selection is not strictly an interview. George Stoney wrote it from notes taken at the time of Wolfe's appearance before a student group at Chapel Hill in January, 1937 (see the interview in Raleigh News and Observer, January 22, 1937, earlier in this collection), long after the occasion. It was titled "Eugene Returns to Pulpit Hill: Reminiscences of a 'Wolverine.'"

I once knew a boy who never left home for a single night without his copy of *Look Homeward, Angel*. Even when he went camping he would wrap it carefully in a flannel scarf and put it in the bottom of his knapsack. I was almost as bad myself. From the day a high school English teacher read aloud "The Death of Ben" I kept the volumes of the master close beside my bed and read a bit each night.

A couple of years ago there was a group of us Wolfe enthusiasts at the Hill; "Wolverines" we called ourselves. We searched the town for things he had alluded to, took courses under professors because he happened to have mentioned them, pumped every one who had ever seen him for stories. We were no formal group. Each worked out his theories about Wolfe's "literary development," his "trends," his "influences," by himself. We noted down our friends and professors—material for *our* Look Homeward's. We wrote of "the thousand faces, the ten thousand mouths . . ." in foolish effort to approximate his style. We tried to taste, smell, see with his catholicity and acuteness. We stretched our puny powers out until they ached in futile mummery of him—giant that he was, all-absorbing filter for sensations. At least one disciple, a gifted linguistic scholar and poet, nearly wrecked his slight frame trying to copy, in realistic detail, the eating, drinking and whoring habits of our master.

Then Eugene came back to Pulpit Hill. Tremendous, flabby, stuttering, homesick, still a boy at thirty-six, his warm brown eyes

pleaded forgiveness; his stumbling heavy lips blubbered sentimentalities about how good it was to be back. I met him first back of
the library. He pushed his shoulders through the narrow car door
and wrapped my hand in his soft, sweaty paw as in a blanket. My
heart was in my throat, clogging every word of that hundred-times-
rehearsed sentence of greeting. Then Wolfe stood erect beside Dean
"Shorty" Spruill, who was his host, and I laughed. This great-jawed,
misshapen giant whose clothes and flesh hung down in formless
ugliness, whose meaty mouth fell open to emit a spluttering, high-
keyed greeting, stood matched with the Dean's trim midget figure,
with its tight-skinned face and narrow, blinking eyes. Oh what master
of grotesque could have planned that combination!

Wolfe looked at me, then down a foot or more to where the top of
Shorty's hair began, and laughed too. I forgot my prepared greeting.
(And I can't recall it now, except that it said something about a "master builder of the world-soul" and it rimed.) Instead I said I hoped he
would let us boys get together with him some time for a talk.

"Yeahhh," he stuttered out eagerly. "I'd c-c-certainly like to. M-m-
mister Phillips Russell has asked me to s-s-say s-s-something to his
class in writing this morning. Ah-ah-g-gosh, I don't know w-w-what
I can tell 'em. I-I-I-I t-told him I couldn't make a speech, but he
seemed to think it was all right anyway. I-I-I just hope th-they will
keep asking questions so I can keep going somehow. . . ."

It was a restless, eager hundred students waiting in the Archeol-
ogy theater of Murphey hall, the Wolverines, the curious, and that
year's "intellectuals," who tried to hide their excitement under superior disdain. Half a period long we waited before he came. Mr.
Russell's usual provocativeness seemed dull, impotent. The "intellectuals" talked among themselves of Wolfe's "verbosity," his "lack of literary discipline." We Wolverines smirked at them and chewed our
pencils.

He came at last, stumbling down the stairs, a flushed, sweaty face
and a hoarse mutter of apology. He fumbled with his coat button,
whispered almost pleadingly to Mr. Russell and then turned toward
the class. He stretched his heavy frame, photographed the assem-

blage in one long stare and then dropped his head and drew circles on the floor with his feet. "I-I-I th-thought I was c-c-coming to sit in on a class-ss," he said. "I-I-I didn't. . . . Wh-when I was here t-there weren't any more than th-th-this in school." He stumbled on a few sentences longer in this same fashion, as though some physical disorder was inhibiting the flow of words.

He was scared. The great devourer of ten thousand nights was cowed by a hundred undergraduates. But somehow the restlessness, the squirming embarrassment that usually comes over an audience when someone is tongue-tied with fright did not come. Perhaps it was because he never started with assurance and then faltered. Or perhaps it was because Wolfe was so homely-humble, yet so enormous that it was impossible to feel sorry for him. Instead a kind of warm kindredship spread all around. The "intellectuals" dropped their haughtiness and began to smile. The tenseness went out of the rest of us. A quiet friendly laugh arose. He looked up smiling, grateful, warming every face with his eyes' glow.

"It's s-s-s-soo good to be back," he said naively, his words beginning to flow more freely now. "I was just telling Shorty here how much of it all I had forgotten. The color of our Carolina clay. I never remembered it was so red before. And the dogwood and the broom sage, I-I-I-I. . . ." He walked up and down in front of the class, three strides and back, coursing his plentiful hair with hands that seemed never to be still.

"I was j-just telling Shorty here this morning how things have changed. Why when we were here all this part down below Old South was nothing but blackberry thicket. Why God-a-mighty. . . ." His voice was thick and Southern still. On he talked then, of the old days, of how good it was to be in one's home state again—sentimentalities full of wordless pleadings for forgiveness. And this pleading was in every gesture, every movement. Somehow he felt he had personally put a great curse upon this state he loved and now he was humiliating himself, truly penitent. He disdained the city folk. "They argue long and loud but they can't really talk like people in the South." He said he was going back to Asheville to offer up his humility as an appeasement for the blight he had put on that place. Then—for he knew he could never be accepted in Asheville again, holy of holies that it might be—he planned to move with his mother out into the hills of Yancey County and write of the homely wisdom he found there.

("Did you really mean that, about going back to live in Yancey County?" I asked Wolfe a year later as we cracked pecans together in his barnlike rooms at Hotel Chelsea in New York. He smiled a little bitterly.

"I did then. But going back taught me this one thing. A man can't go back home again. He is like a fledgling gull that leaves his warm, familiar nest to try his wings. When he flies back he finds what he had left is but sticks and mud. I want to visit North Carolina often. I want to do another book on Asheville. . . . But I could never go back there to live, back there or any other place for long. I have to move. My home is in my work, now, and if I'm still too long the words get knotted up inside. That's why I love this city. It's always moving, shaking, never still. Oh yes it's ugly, cruel, raw but still I like it. . . .")

From his words that January morning no one would have guessed he ever wanted to see another subway. "E-everybody's been so kind. Why l-last night Misses Spruill p-put a steak in front of me at least a foot square and then said, 'I'm sorry but it's the biggest one the butcher had.' Well, God, I like to eat but. . . ."

The class was eager now for other things. We peppered him with questions: How did he write? Did he take notes? . . .

Yes, he did take notes, he said; not very elaborate ones, often nothing more than a sentence on an envelope. He never used the note-book-in-hand method his friend Sinclair Lewis did, who copied down even the notations a man made on his date calendar. Wolfe himself did not take notes until his experience had "aged" a bit, and the incident stood out with its essential details uncluttered by irrelevances. Every writer, he said, had a certain aging period, a certain length of time it took him to shape things in his mind. "Generally I have to wait about a year before I can write about a thing."

"And do you mean that you write directly about the things you do and see?" asked one of the "intellectuals" in mock astonishment. Wolfe flushed. The bottom of the sin he was trying to absolve had been bared most cruelly. He squirmed, and sent a pleading look toward the questioner. But that acid little boy was heartless. "Do you," he insisted, turning the knife in the wound, "use actual people and events for your material?" Wolfe faced the questioner squarely now, his eyebrows bristling and his heavy lower lip thrust forward almost in anger. In his voice, however, there was not so much of defiance as of pleading.

"A writer has to use what he has to use! Every writer writes more or less out of his own experience. Where else could he go for his material? Unless he gets it out of books, and that is just copying the experience of other people." He did not parry the point, however. He knew where it pointed. "I made the same mistake at first that so many young writers make. I thought that when I wrote a story about a grocer's wife from Kannapolis, say, who was the mistress of a banker, I had to say she came from Kannapolis and that she was a grocer's wife or it was not real. . . ." And then he went on to give that magnificent defence of himself and his writing methods that appeared in *The Story of a Novel* and he told it in almost the same phrases.

This repeating of things he had written was customary with him, I learned from later talks. He had three ways of talking. The first was that haltering, almost unintelligible stutter with which he spoke to people at literary teas (and how he hated them!), haughty servants, and strangers, and which filled the first ten minutes of almost every conversation. If he was comfortable in a conversation, the second way of speaking would soon replace the first; heavy, swift, full of the gurgle of rich laughter, the enthusiasm for life; manly and full of confidence, almost a swagger. The third was his literary voice. It often interrupted his second voice when he was in the mood. Great torrents of words flowed out in a passion. It was lyric often, supple to the every mood that passed through his being. Or it was dramatic,

catching the banter and cadence of street speech and tossing it about
with scornful agility. Or it was epic and marked in elephantine stresses
those sentences that swept whole continents into a single concept.

These three voices were as distinct and fuseless as the two which
an adolescent struggles with, and the change from one to another
came with the same grotesque suddenness. That day we felt them
when his self-defence flowed out. Warmed by this torrent, we were
eager for more.

"And how do you cut?" I asked, knowing this was another sore
point with him but willing to risk his anger if this prick would start
another such flowing. He flushed again and stammered.

"I-I-I . . . well-ll I guess that's my weak point there," he blurted
out. Then he told of some of the heartrendings he had felt when hundreds of thousands of words had to be discarded from the manuscript
of *Look Homeward, Angel.* "It's not that I want people to spend time
reading what I write . . . why God I wish I could splatter a hundred
thousand words on that wall there so people could read them all at
once!" His arm shot out in a sweeping arc and he nearly shouted the
words.

"But I've learned now," he went on more quietly, "that you never
really lose anything. It's all your experience and they can't cut that.
What they throw away one time you can use again." His voice caressed
those bereavements he had just recalled and was full of soothing for
us who would suffer as he had. We Wolverines were entranced.
Hanging on every word we would not let him rest. "What do you
read? What plan do you write by? Who influenced you most?" He
spoke of Milton, Keats, the Bible and then more directly James Joyce.

"What about Walt Whitman?" we asked. He laughed.

"After I found so many critics saying I was rewriting his stuff I
decided I had better go back and read up on him, to see what I had
missed. I found a great poet and now perhaps I am influenced by
him. . . . Of course I don't think any young writer ought to copy anyone's style directly, but I do think he ought to read. After all that is
where he finds words. And he is bound to be influenced to some degree in his writings by what he reads, first by one author and then

another. Gradually they will help shape his own style. I don't believe two men can use the same style because no two men think exactly the same way. A man can't consciously shape his own style either. He must write as he feels and thinks; his style will shape itself, whatever is necessary for that man."

"And do critics and reviewers affect your writing?" came another question, though the bell for lunch had long since rung.

"Not directly I don't think, but indirectly I guess they do. I guess I care too much what people think and write about me. I remember talking once with Ernest Hemingway, the novelist, when we were at a dinner of prominent writers. 'Why you don't read reviews, do you!' he said." Wolfe's voice rose in feigned scorn, then broke out loudly, "You just bet I do! And if I knew Miss Suzy Stross was writing a piece about me in the Skunkstown, Ohio, Busy Bee I'd stay up all night to get the first copy off the press."

Late into the lunch hour we stood around him with our questions and it was obvious that he was just warming up. He rested his fat haunches on the desk, his feet still flat on the floor, and answered without hesitation. He was eager to be liked; there was no reserve or feeling of importance in his manner, no effort to inspire respect. (Physically large men can dispense with such.) At thirty-six he was our eager boy companion. Circled around him we Wolverines found the man whose spirit had fed our lives, no great Apollo but an image of ourselves—multiplied by two in size, by ten in appetites and passions and by a thousand in expressiveness.

Yet he was ourselves. His warm eyes told us that. Enormous and complex, as supple and revealing as his voice, they, too, had a triple nature. I watched them once when he was looking about the manuscript-littered room at Hotel Chelsea where he spent a year and a half of the hardest working period of his life. They shrank to tiny sparks, and with quick darting movements they picked out each corner and shadow in the room. Again, as that day when we crowded around him, they could take on a general focus—a general focus to look at a person or a group and to draw them around him as to an open fire, bathed in their soft amber light. Then at times, as once or twice that day I recalled them doing, they would lose their focus and, dilating, would, like two great yellow floodlights, seem to cover the whole room at once. One felt engulfed, as in a great bear hug.

It took the autograph hunters to break the spell of this companion circle. At their pink-ribboned books he was the stuttering, fumbling giant again. After them I too, embarrassed and apologizing over much, held up my treasured volumes, well preserved in dust jackets but obviously well read. He fondled them and wrote: "For George Stoney, Thomas Wolfe"—a bold, straight scrawl.

For two more days Wolfe was in Chapel Hill. Mrs. Spruill had one of those literary teas that he cursed so much in private. Only faculty members and their wives were invited. They took him to see "Buck Benson" [William Stanly "Bully" Bernard] and he passed the evening with the "old philosopher" [Horace Williams]. One night some of his college mates, now faculty members and businessmen, gathered around the bottle out at Phillips Russell's. At four A.M. he was talking impetuously, when the rest of them called for the calf rope.

Of all this we Wolverines only heard rumors. We ached to be in on all of it. Yet at heart we were content with what we had experienced. How rare a privilege it had been. We, as youths, had seen our hero, known him and he still remained a man.

After graduating from the university, George Stoney went to New York, where he visited Wolfe occasionally. During that last weekend at the Chelsea Hotel before setting out for the West, Wolfe had his young admirer in to type for him. Stoney's career has been in film production. He is now professor of film and video at Washington Square College, New York University.

In other reports of Wolfe's classroom appearance at Chapel Hill, Oliver Crawley (Raleigh State, February 27, 1937, p. 9) wrote that Wolfe said: "I like to write about people talking. I love food and I always mention the inside of a refrigerator—what the characters had for dinner, or something along that line. I don't like to cut material in my writing. I seem to always have too much, whereas some writers such as Hemingway claim they can't get enough." Irene Wright (Asheville Citizen, *January 30, 1937) told how Wolfe, in high spirits, "confessed to a habit of using eight adjectives where only one would do, and expressed a hope that some day he would use only four where two are enough." An anonymous reporter (Greensboro* Daily News, *January 23, 1937) recorded that when asked "whether he thought literature during the next 25 years would lean more toward realism or swing back toward romanticism," Wolfe replied:*

"I would prefer to answer that this way. I think that in America the lid is going to be off, that we are going to pull the stops, as they say. And please don't misunderstand me. I don't mean that our writers are going to be offensive. But more and more they are going to tell the story of American life as they see it and let the quips fall where they may." Obviously Wolfe felt that he had showed them how it could be done.

Index

Lafayette, Indiana, 102
Lancaster, Pennsylvania, 7
Langley Field, Virginia, 14
Lanzinger, Klaus, 69
Ledig-Rowohlt, Heinz M., 65
Letters of Thomas Wolfe, The, 27, 120
Letters of Thomas Wolfe to His Mother, The, 21
Lewis, Sinclair, 4, 8, 12, 13, 28, 30, 71, 75, 124
Lexer, Dr. Geheimrat, 68
Lindbergh, Charles, 68
London. *See* England
"Look Homeward, Angel," 117
Look Homeward, Angel: publication by Scribner's of, 1, 2, 6, 21, 29, 31, 60, 80, 83, 84, 87, 112, 116–17, 118, 121; writing of, 3, 6, 10, 14, 22, 24, 35, 54, 70, 78, 81, 109, 126; copies inscribed of, 4, 127; reception in Asheville of, 5, 13, 55, 71, 76, 82, 85, 86, 92, 124; significance of title of, 8, 10; form of, 18; German translation of, 27, 31; theme of, 30, 93
"Lost Boy, The," 46
Lowell, James Russell, 24
Ludendorff, General Erich, 28

McCoy, George, 86
McDermott, "Fatty," 73
McNeal, Blanche Young, 37
Magi, Aldo P., 20
Maine, 15, 20
Mardi Gras, 70
Marion, Virginia, 97
Maugham, W. Somerset, 23
Metcalfe, Ralph, 65, 67
Miller, Edward M., 42, 107, 110, 111
Miller, Mrs. Edward M., 107
Milton, John, 8, 126
Mississippi River, 73
Mitchell, Margaret, 77, 85, 109
Montana, 107
Munich, Germany, 67, 116. *See also* Oktoberfest

New England, 61
New Orleans, Louisiana, 70, 73, 75, 77
New Orleans *Item*, 73
New Orleans *Times-Picayune*, 73

New Orleans *Times-Picayune New Orleans States*, 70
Newport News, Virginia, 14
New Republic, 81, 88
New York, New York, 5, 25, 27, 31, 70, 74, 84, 87, 89, 97, 99
New York *Herald Tribune*, 21, 50, 54, 58
New York *Post*, 58
New York *Times*, 11, 31
New York University, 1, 2, 9, 16, 56
New York University *Daily News*, 1
New York *World*, 1
Norfolk, Virginia, 14
"North Carolina, The" (St. Louis), 46
North Carolina, University of. *See* Wolfe, Thomas, education of
North State Fitting School. *See* Wolfe, Thomas, education of
Norway, 118
Notebooks of Thomas Wolfe, The, 27
Note on Experts, A, 25
Nowell, Elizabeth, 21, 27, 33, 50, 70, 108, 111, 119, 120
Nuremburg, Germany, 67

October Fair, 6, 9, 14, 20, 51, 56, 81, 85
Of Time and the River: publication by Scribner's of, 22, 23, 27, 29, 30, 31, 32, 46, 49, 52, 54, 62, 71, 77, 80, 84, 85, 93, 112, 118; writing of, 22, 51, 55, 81, 109; condensation of, 31; excisions from, 118
Oktoberfest, 65, 67
"O Lost," 117
Olympia, Washington, 111
Olympic Games, 65, 67, 109
Olympic Peninsula, Washington, 108
Oregon, 51, 105, 107
Oregon State Motor Association, 107, 110
Oteen, North Carolina, 91, 92, 93
Owens, Jesse, 65, 67

Pacific End, 23
Paris, France, 17, 27, 32, 61, 69, 104, 113
Parker, Dorothy, 49
Pennsylvania, 7